Project Risk Analysis and Management Guide

Second edition

apmKNOWLEDGE

Association for Project Management
Ibis House, Regent Park
Summerleys Road
Princes Risborough
Buckinghamshire
HP27 9LE

British Library Cataloguing in Publication Data is available

ISBN 1-903494-12-5

Typeset in 10/12pt Palatino by Genesis Typesetting, Rochester, Kent
Printed and bound by Hobbs the Printers, Hampshire
Cover design by Dan Bura at Fountainhead, Middlesex
Copy editor Linda Cayford
Proof-reader Valerie Hall

Contents

Contents

Contents

List of figures

List of figures

List of tables

Notes on the contributors

John Bartlett has over 30 years' expertise in business strategy formulation, programme management and project management. His particular specialities are business and IT risk management, project quality management, and the specification and delivery of business change. His published books include *Management of Programme Risk, Managing Risk for Projects and Programmes* and *Managing Programmes of Business Change*. He is a Fellow of the Association for Project Management, an APM Certificated Project Manager, a member of the US Project Management Institute and a Fellow of the Royal Society for the Encouragement of Arts, Manufactures and Commerce.

Chris Chapman has been Professor of Management Science at the University of Southampton, since 1986. He was founding Chair of the Association for Project Management's Project Risk Management Specific Interest Group from 1986–91. Since 1975, his consulting and research have focussed on risk management, with an extensive list of well-known clients in the United States, Canada and the United Kingdom. His publications include six books, twenty book chapters and 44 refereed academic journal papers. *Project Risk Management: Processes, Techniques and Insights*, the 2003 second edition of a book first published in 1997, with Stephen Ward, is a standard in the field.

Paul Close, BSc, is a risk consultant at Fujitsu Services. He has provided consultancy in information technology bids, projects and services in the United Kingdom and internationally. Paul has also delivered risk consultancy externally to several of Fujitsu's customers. He is a co-author of Fujitsu's risk management process, toolkit and training and has delivered risk management training to several hundred staff across Europe.

Karl Davey, CEng, MIEE, of Strategic Thought Limited, is the product manager for the 'Active Risk Manager' (ARM), a leading web based integrated risk management system. Karl has over 11 years' extensive experience in the application of proactive risk management across organisations and on major projects.

Karl is experienced in developing methods to promote risk management buy-in within organisations through increasing communication and participation. Other process developments he has been involved with include the effective use of risk contingency for capital works programmes and the use of risk management to support PFI/PPP. He has provided proven risk management training for universities and other major organisations in the United Kingdom, the United States, Australia, and Japan. Karl has also been responsible for writing the risk management chapter in the Association for Project Management's *Project Management Pathways* publication.

Piyush Desai has practised risk management on projects for more than ten years, after graduating in Construction Management at the University of Westminster. He started his career as a project planner with Cyril Sweett Project Consultants and progressed into risk management by considering schedule risks on projects. After joining management consultant Vector Management Limited, Piyush introduced risk management processes for various clients, including British Airways and employed these methods at the Terminal 5 project at Heathrow Airport. In 2003, Piyush joined Turner & Townsend Management Solutions, where he has contributed extensively to the management of risks on the Home Office headquarters project.

Ron Gerdes is Head of Risk Management with BMT Reliability Consultants Limited. He has been responsible for the development of BMT Reliability Consultants' capability in risk management and safety including the development of methods, tools and training. Ron's qualifications include degrees in Cybernetics and Artificial Intelligence and he is a Member of the APM. He has an interest in all aspects of risk management, including effective risk management within organisations and corporate governance. Ron has worked in the United Kingdom, the United States and Europe and his experience includes civil aircraft, military aircraft, industrial, rail, road transport and shipping sectors.

Heather Groom has more than 15 years' practical experience of project risk management. Having graduated in Applied Statistics from Sheffield in 1982, she later joined the British Aircraft Corporation, playing a 'risk manager' role on a major defence contract and spent four years with hands-on experience of cost and schedule Monte Carlo Modelling. In 1995, Heather established a new role within the company, forming a Centre of Excellence for Risk Management, responsible for process, training, tools, and ad-hoc risk services. Heather has provided a well-used service across all project teams and gained an invaluable insight into the behavioural aspects of risk management. When the guided weapons division of British Aerospace merged with Matra Defence of France, and then Alenia of Italy to ultimately form MBDA, Heather exchanged best practice on risk management with her European colleagues.

In 1993, Heather formed her own company and began work as a risk management consultant, doing much of her work as an associate of Risk Decisions Ltd, focusing both on risk management tools and process.

Dr David Hillson, FAPM, FIRM, PMP, is an international risk management consultant and Director of Risk Doctor & Partners. He is a popular conference speaker and an author on risk. David is recognised internationally as a leading thinker and practitioner in the risk field and has made several innovative contributions to improving risk management, notably the inclusion of proactive opportunity management within the risk process. David is a Fellow of the Association for Project Management and a past Chairman of its Risk Management Specific Interest Group. He is a founder member of the Project Management Institute (PMI) Risk SIG and received the PMI Distinguished Contribution Award in 2002.

Martin Hopkinson, BSc (Physics), APMP, is a Principal Consultant with HVR Consulting Services, specialising in risk management, project planning and the governance of project management. Prior to his five years with HVR, he gained 14 years' project management experience in industry. He has led the risk management process on several multi-billion pound projects. Martin is also the lead developer for two tools pioneered by HVR: the Risk Maturity Model (RMM) and the Top-Down Risk Model. The RMM has been used for formal risk management capability assessments on more than 100 projects and has been adopted as a strategic tool by the Defence Procurement Agency in the United Kingdom.

Emma Major, BEng (Hons), MSc (Eng), MAPM, MPMI, MIAF, IVM, AMICE, is an experienced project manager with extensive experience delivering risk management, value management, partnering improvement, procedure optimisation and strategy development. She currently owns and operates her own consultancy, Major Value Consultancy Ltd, delivering these services to United Kingdom construction clients, county councils, consultancies and contractors. She has trained over 300 project managers in risk management and facilitated over 250 workshops over the last five years. Emma has presented three papers on risk management: one for the PMI Congress Europe 2003, introducing the idea of combining value and risk management; the second for the Hong Kong Institute of Value Management, which discussed project stakeholder uncertainties; and the third for the PMI College of Scheduling, discussing the identification and management of uncertainties on project schedules.

Ken Newland is an experienced risk and project management consultant. He initially qualified in Electronics/ Radio Communications with the GPO. In 1969 he joined Ferranti, progressing from design through programme management to business development and department management. In 1991, he joined the consultancy Quintec Associates, becoming its managing director later that year. Personal assignments included risk management for the UK's Ministry of Defence and for industry. He has chaired the Association for Project Management's Risk Management Specific Interest Group, and was an author and editor for the first edition of the *Project Risk Analysis* *and Management Guide* (the PRAM Guide). Recently, he led the Thales Work-stream for Risk Management, setting out the practices for the whole Thales Company.

Dr Stephen Simister, Bsc (Hons), PhD, MRICS, FAPM, CVM, is a consultant and lecturer in project management and a director of his own company, Oxford Management & Research Limited. Stephen has been involved with project management for over 20 years, initially in the construction industry and latterly in information technology, pharmaceuticals, defence and rail. As a fellow of the Association for Project Management, Stephen is chairman of the Contracts & Procurement Specific Interest Group, which provides a focal point for all contract and procurement issues in relation to project management. He is also a chartered building surveyor with the Royal Institution of Chartered Surveyors and sits on their construction procurement panel. Stephen lectures at a number of European universities and has written extensively on the subject of project management and risk management.

Margaret Greenwood, Peter Campbell (Defence Procurement Agency) and **Professor Terry Williams** (University of Strathclyde) also contributed material to this the second edition of the *Project Risk Analysis and Management Guide*.

Foreword to the second edition

Since the publication of the first edition of the *PRAM Guide* in 1997, there has been continual refinement of the techniques and concepts of risk management, coupled with a raised corporate view of risk management practice resulting from considerations of corporate governance. However, many of the basic concepts of risk management remain the same as they were in 1997.

Our challenge in updating the *Guide* was to maintain the original book's balance between the basic and more advanced concepts while introducing ideas developed or refined since 1997. We have tried to achieve this through a team that combines many of the original *PRAM* authors with several new names. This approach has not always worked as expected; in some cases, it has been the old guard who have argued vigorously for greater change and the new blood who have advocated a more conservative approach. We leave it to the reader to decide whether we have been successful in this challenge.

We have restructured the *Guide* slightly, separating out benefits into a self-contained chapter and providing an expanded glossary. We have also added a selective list of further reading. Throughout the *Guide* we have shown the applicability of risk management to threats and opportunities, an approach foreseen in the 1997 version of the *PRAM Guide*, but not expanded. Chapter 1 fully describes the content and structure of the 2004 version, but the major changes are briefly described below.

In Chapter 2, 'Benefits', we have added the benefits of risk management in projects to the wider perspectives of the organisation.

We have reorganised the process in Chapters 3 and 4 to show how project risk in general, as well as individual risk events, can be addressed so that fundamental causes of risk in scope and solution can be dealt with at the appropriate point in the project life cycle, as well as the immediate causes of specific risk events. We have also separated the management of the risk process from the management of the risks themselves, and shown how a multiple looping approach, although more complex to describe than a simple sequential process, provides greater focus on the uncertainties that matter and how to respond to them. This approach is intended to lead to a more effective application of the risk management process and to produce a risk-efficient set of responses.

We have extended the scope of Chapter 5 on organisation and control to reflect the influence of corporate governance best practice and to show how project risk management connects to programme or corporate risk management. We have also expanded the risk specialist roles to reflect typical styles in which risk skills are applied to projects.

Foreword to the second edition

In Chapter 6, 'Behavioural Influences', now a chapter on its own, we have expanded on the importance of 'softer' issues of personal perception and behaviour and external influences on successful risk management, along with some approaches to address them.

Chapter 7, 'Application of PRAM', focuses on a greater awareness of the business perspective, including the business case for the project, the existing process structure and risk maturity of the organisation, in order to define appropriate objectives and to measure the effectiveness of risk management for the project and the business.

We have restructured and expanded Chapter 8 on 'Tools and Techniques', and the associated Appendix, 'Using Risk Management Techniques', to reflect the richer choice available today and the increasing trend towards managing opportunities in the same process as threats.

The authors of the second edition of the *PRAM Guide* are as follows:

Foreword and Introduction	Paul Close (Fujitsu Services Ltd.)
Benefits	Heather Groom
Principles	Dr David Hillson (Risk Doctor Ltd.)
The PRAM Process	Professor Chris Chapman (University of Southampton) Dr Steve Simister (OMR Ltd.)
Organisation and Control	John Bartlett (Great Stave) Ron Gerdes (BMT Reliability Consultants)
Behavioural Influences	Heather Groom, with contributions from Margaret Greenwood
Application of PRAM	Ken Newland (Quintec Associates Ltd) Karl Davey (Strategic Thought Ltd) Piyush Desai (Turner and Townsend Management Solutions)
Tools and Techniques	Martin Hopkinson (HVR Consulting Services Ltd)
Appendix	Edited by Martin Hopkinson with contributions from: Dr David Hillson Professor Chris Chapman Emma Major (Major Value Consultancy) Professor Terry Williams (University of Strathclyde) Peter Campbell (Defence Procurement Agency)
Glossary	Edited by Paul Close (Fujitsu Services)
Further Reading	Edited by Dr David Hillson (Risk Doctor Ltd.)

We would like to thank Margaret Greenwood (who contributed material to Chapter 6) and, of course, the editors, authors, and the steering group of the first edition of the *Guide*, many of whom have contributed in same way to this second edition of the *Project Risk Analysis and Management Guide*.

The development and production of the second edition was project-managed by Paul Close and directed by a steering group comprising Dr David Hillson (Risk Doctor Ltd), Guy Hindley (BAE Systems), Tom Teixeira (Strategic Thought Ltd) and Deborah Vogwell (Davis Langdon and Everest).

We would like to thank the Review Team for their constructive and sharp-eyed comments. They were Peter Curtis (Ladymead Projects), Michael Hepworth, Paul Jobling (Parsons Brinckerhoff), Tony McDonald (BMT Sigma Ltd), Philip Rawlings (Euro Log Ltd) and Peter Simon (Lucidus Consulting).

We would also like to thank the officers of the Specific Interest Group on Project Risk and the APM for their support during the writing and production of the second edition. Special thanks to Simon Jackson (secretary of the Risk Management Specific Interest Group) and Jeremy Harrison (chairman of the Risk Management Specific Interest Group), and Ingmar Folkmans of APM Publishing.

We would like to thank Powersim Limited for their kind permission to use the influence diagrams in the Appendix, which were created using the Powersim system dynamics package, Powersim Studio.

Paul Close
June 2004

Foreword to the first edition

For many years the Association for Project Management's Specific Interest Group on Project Risk (Risk SIG) debated the merits of producing a document that reflected its vast wealth of knowledge. No one thought it would be easy to gain consensus and achieve this, and indeed it was not. However, this document represents the culmination of an initiative first started in late 1994 to produce a detailed guide to project risk analysis and management.

The *Guide* has been produced by the efforts of numerous members of the Risk SIG. Many of those who have attended meetings of the SIG during the production period of the document can feel that they have contributed to some degree. But, as is normal in the production of a 'document by committee', there is always more effort put in by only a few individuals.

In early 1995 a representative 'steering group' was formed to agree the format of the *Guide*, to act as a sounding board for thoughts and musings and as a first-pass proof reader. Chapters were authored by individual members of this steering group as detailed below. The editing has been undertaken by myself with considerable assistance from David Hillson and Ken Newland. Everyone associated with the *Guide* has given their time free of charge and, on behalf of the Risk SIG, I would like to thank both them and their parent companies for their generosity in so doing. I would also like to add my personal thanks to all of them, and in particular to my co-editors, for pushing me to finalise the document.

Individual chapter authors:

Introduction	Ken Newland (Quintec Associates Ltd)
Principles	Martin Mays (MM Associates)
The PRAM process	Professor Chris Chapman (University of Southampton)
Organisation and control	Ron Gerdes (BMT Reliability Consultants)
Expectations and behaviour	Ken Newland
Techniques	Dr David Hillson (HVR Consulting Services) and Philip Rawlings (Euro Log)
Implementation of PRAM	Catriona Norris (KPMG) and Ken Newland
Appendix	David Vose (DVRA) and David Hillson

Other steering group members:
Paul Best (Frazer-Nash Consultancy)
Adrian Cowderoy (City University)
Keith Gray (BAe Defence)
Dr Stephen Grey (ICL)
Heather Groom (BAe Defence)
Ross Hayes (University of Birmingham)
Paul Jobling (Mouchel Management)
Grahame Owen (IBM)
Frances Scarff (CCTA)
Martin Thomas (4D Management Consultancy)
Valerie Evans (MoD(PE))

I hope that this document, now known as *The Association for Project Management Project Risk Analysis and Management Guide* or *PRAM Guide* will be of use to anyone and everyone with an interest in the subject. It has been structured in such a way that both a novice and an expert, and all abilities between, can learn from it. The novice should be able to read at least the early chapters and gain an insight into the subject, and an expert can hone their knowledge of the more detailed analytical techniques by reading the Appendix.

No direct references are listed or quoted in the document and there is no advice given on the numerous and varied supporting software packages that are available. This has been deliberate. The information given in the text is considered by the authors and editors to be in the public domain. Software systems continue to change and therefore to include references today would date the *Guide* immediately. We also felt that it was unwise and unfair of us to recommend any software when we are unaware of the total market. However, should the reader require further bibliographic references or a list of available software (as up-to-date as possible) these can be obtained directly from the website of the Association for Project Management.

It must be remembered that PRAM is not a panacea for all project management failings, but it is an integral part of good project management. To emphasise this point I would like to quote a former member of the Risk SIG, Paul Rook, who died before this document was completed. I believe Paul's definition of risk management summarises the prime motivation behind the implementation of the PRAM process.

> *'Project risk management does not guarantee success but has the primary goal of identifying and responding to potential problems with sufficient lead time to avoid crises, so that it is possible for project management to achieve its goal of a successful project which meets its targets.'*

Peter Simon
October 1997

1

Introduction

THE PURPOSE OF THE *GUIDE*

Risk is present in all projects whatever their nature, although some projects are inherently more 'risky' than others because of the nature of their task, the technology on which they are based, or the environment in which they are undertaken. A formal approach to risk management in projects is often demanded by customers or by the governance requirements of the organisation itself. As there are many possible approaches to risk management, and many tools and techniques to support these approaches, it is often difficult for the inexperienced project manager to determine which approach would be most appropriate to meet his project's needs.

The *PRAM Guide* describes a systematic and disciplined approach to controlling risk that can be used to help improve the success of projects. It sets out methods for the identification and recording of risks, highlighting the consequences and establishing appropriate management action. The *Guide* does not prescribe a system that project managers can adopt without careful thought; it will still be necessary to study other risk methods and techniques and to develop judgement through personal experience. Successful project managers know that they must develop an approach to each project that is appropriate for the purpose and which makes full use of the team's strengths and the inherent qualities of the project and its environment. It must also reflect the project manager's own individual style of management. There are, as always, no short-cuts to good management.

This latest edition of the *Guide* aims to assist project managers and risk practitioners by describing a range of approaches and techniques that are being used by their peers, and from which they may choose to suit their own particular circumstances.

This Introduction describes some of the issues and choices with respect to possible approaches and then goes on to outline the structure of the *Guide*.

APPROACHES TO RISK MANAGEMENT IN PROJECTS

A successfully managed project is one that achieves its stated objectives in the most effective manner possible. No project manager would attempt to run a project without giving the disciplines of quality management, planning and financial management detailed attention; the same is true of risk management. However, the benefits of risk management may be achieved in many ways.

Many project managers still see risk management as a rearguard action to protect the project from its own fears. In some cases, it is only applied superficially in order to comply with internal company rules or meet client expectations.

Simply managing to lowest cost – a typical scenario resulting from competitive fixed-price bids or unenlightened project sponsors – potentially leaves the project exposed to inherent risks. Identifying those risks and making mitigation plans in the form of alternative paths, action plans or 'a contingency fund' go some way towards dealing with the risk, but such an approach can be too reactive in that the mitigation plan is invoked only when the potential threat has become an issue, and opportunities (that is, risks with a positive impact) are not actively pursued.

If a project team is to be successful it cannot rely on the absence of problems but must predict and manage the inherent risks so that, when problems do occur, they can be overcome and, when opportunities arise, the benefits are maximised. A successful project manager is undoubtedly also a good risk manager who not only controls project risks to avoid 'management-by-crisis', but is also aware of opportunities and is ready to exploit them as they arise.

The effective management of risks will reduce the requirement for contingency planning, leading to more competitive bids, more profitable projects and more satisfied customers. This 'risk-efficient' approach acknowledges that proactive and judicious spending of some of the risk budget (time and/or cost) before risks occur offers the project manager the opportunity to exercise full management control over those potential events.

The net effect is to make the project far less susceptible to chance in that threats are rendered less critical in impact, or even eliminated altogether, and significant opportunities are actively pursued and realised. As a consequence, the project is less exposed to 'crisis' situations, and thus the project team is less stressed, more confident and is better able to apply its skills. The net result is a project that is more likely to succeed in achieving its stated objectives within agreed time and cost budgets and a customer who is more relaxed and happy.

Project risk analysis and management, as described in this *Guide*, is in many respects a formalisation of the common sense that project managers usually apply to their projects. It is not a new way of managing and need not require a significant change in the way a project manager thinks or behaves. It is a tool to assist in discharging project responsibilities effectively and in ensuring the fulfilment of project objectives. Although project risk analysis and management has a clearly defined formal structure, it cannot be applied mechanically – it should not be seen as a 'painting by numbers' approach. Most experienced risk practitioners understand this, but formal statements of risk methodologies do not always make this important point clear. Creativity, lateral thinking and an understanding of the domain or environment in which the project is taking place are crucial to successful risk management.

Project risk analysis and management is often concerned with extremely complex risk issues, so a complex method is the last thing that is needed. Accordingly, the method described in this *Guide* has been kept as simple as possible, while nevertheless fully encompassing all the various methods and viewpoints known to the authors that contribute to the comprehensive analysis and management of risk. This means that this *Guide* does not knowingly exclude any approaches that are currently being used successfully.

At its most fundamental level, risk management is extremely simple. The risks (both threats and opportunities) are identified, a prediction is made on how likely they are and the extent of their impact, decisions are taken on what to do about them, and then those decisions are implemented. At a more complex level, overall risk outcomes (rather than individual risk events) are identified and strategies devised to manage these outcomes by, for instance, changing the project approach, solution, timescales, basis of contract or even the scope of the project. This increased complexity is generally rewarded by a significantly improved performance against objectives.

THE STRUCTURE OF THIS *GUIDE*

Following the Introduction, Chapter 2 'Benefits' shows how a formal approach to risk management helps directly and indirectly to improve the likelihood that a project will be successful.

Chapter 3, 'Principles' offers a high-level definition of the recommended approach to managing risk and introduces the fundamental principles and concepts on which the rest of the *Guide* is based. It also provides a summary of the risk management process, which is expanded in Chapter 4.

Chapter 4, 'The PRAM Process' takes the reader through a number of iterations of the process, demonstrating the changing emphasis as the project progresses and better information becomes available. The approaches described here have all been experienced by members of the APM Risk SIG. Few implementations of risk management need to specifically address every phase and action as presented in this chapter although, to varying degrees, every aspect is present in successful risk management.

Having established the principles and described the process in detail, the *Guide* turns to implementation. Chapter 5, 'Organisation and Control', examines risk management in the context of the project's management and describes how to govern and control risk management activities on the project.

By definition, risk management involves not only most team members, but also other parties, many of whom will not be willing participants when it comes to assessing the nature of risks and how best to deal with them. Understanding this is crucial to successful risk management and is discussed in Chapter 6, 'Behavioural Influences'.

Chapter 7, 'The Application of PRAM', discusses issues concerning the introduction of risk management into the organisation – namely, establishing and sustaining effectiveness, developing capability, measuring success and managing expectations.

Finally, Chapter 8, 'Tools and Techniques' gives a high-level summary of the tools available for implementing a risk management process. These are categorised as identification, quantitative techniques, qualitative techniques, risk control, risk audit and risk management tools. More detailed descriptions of techniques in the first three of these categories are provided in the Appendix, 'Using Risk Management Techniques'.

The *Guide* concludes with a glossary and a list of other publications that may be of interest to the reader in 'Further Reading'.

The principles and objectives of risk management have been widely adopted in recent years. Many government agencies, educated clients and wise contractors now insist on a risk assessment before any contract is placed or undertaken. They also require risk management to be undertaken during execution of the project. Yet, some organisations still take risk management less seriously, perhaps through ignorance or a bad experience. It is hoped that, whatever the reader's circumstances, this *Guide* will go some way towards ensuring that tangible benefits accrue wherever risk management is applied.

2

Benefits

This chapter sets out to identify common benefits of risk management and to point out some of the problems that may be experienced in undertaking project risk management. It is hoped that the reader, armed with this knowledge, will be better able to justify the need for project risk management, and will also develop a more rounded understanding of the issues that can arise.

THE 'HARD' AND 'SOFT' BENEFITS OF RISK MANAGEMENT

It is helpful to divide the many benefits that have been cited by those working in the field of risk management into two categories:

- 'hard' benefits – that is, contingencies, decisions, control, statistics and the like
- 'soft' benefits – that is, people issues which are implicit in some of the 'hard' benefits but which are not usually expressed as benefits in their own right.

The reason for separating these out is that it is relatively easy to express 'hard' benefits and, with enough effort, it is possible to 'measure' them. 'Soft' benefits are much less easy to quantify but, like so many people issues, can give rise to dramatic improvements in performance. Research by the APM Risk SIG in 1996 produced the list of 'hard' and 'soft' benefits shown in Table 2.1, and these are more fully described below. Benefits to other parts of the organisation arising from project risk management follow, and the chapter concludes with a general survey of threats to effective risk management.

'Hard' benefits

H1 Enables better informed and more believable plans, schedules and budgets

All planning is a statement of what needs to be done, together with a prediction of what resources (time, cost, and labour) will be needed to achieve it,

Table 2.1 *The 'hard' and 'soft' benefits of project risk management*

'Hard' Benefits		'Soft' Benefits	
H1	Enables better informed and more believable plans, schedules and budgets	S1	Improves corporate experience and general communication
H2	Increases the likelihood of a project adhering to its schedules and budgets	S2	Leads to a common understanding and improved team spirit
H3	Leads to the use of the most suitable type of contract	S3	Helps distinguish between good luck/good management and bad luck/bad management
H4	Allows a more meaningful assessment of contingencies	S4	Helps develop the ability of staff to assess risks
H5	Discourages the acceptance of financially unsound projects	S5	Focuses project management attention on the real and most important issues
H6	Contributes to the build-up of statistical information to assist in better management of future projects	S6	Facilitates greater risk-taking, thus increasing the benefits gained
H7	Enables a more objective comparison of alternatives	S7	Demonstrates a responsible approach to customers
H8	Identifies, and allocates responsibility to, the best risk owner	S8	Provides a fresh view of the personnel issues in a project

usually expressed as absolutes. Few managers believe that the plans are accurate and, indeed, many treat them as outline guides. The use of risk management to identify risk factors, and to allocate tolerances or contingency in respect of those risks, helps create a more objective description of the tasks and the related budgets and schedules. This gives more credibility to the plans.

H2 Increases the likelihood of a project adhering to its schedules and budgets

Clearly, the more realistic the project's plans (schedules, budgets), the more likely it is that the outcome will reflect those plans. Team members who believe that they have a hopeless task and expect to fail, no matter how well they do, will tend to be demotivated. Giving them achievable targets, in which they can believe, will secure greater levels of commitment leading to a higher probability of success.

In addition, the proactive management of risk will remove some of the threats that would otherwise impact on the project and also realise some of the opportunities to improve the project's outcomes.

H3 *Leads to the use of the most suitable type of contract*

The client in a contractual relationship has many options of contract that he can place on the supplier. The most simple of these are the alternatives of fixed-price and cost-plus financing. A common understanding of the inherent risks within a project can indicate which of these might be most appropriate. Clearly, a high-risk project in a fixed-price environment will cause the supplier to apply high levels of contingency which may eventually work its way into excessive profits if the risks do not arise. In such situations the client might benefit from using cost-plus arrangements so that he can more closely manage the tasks, decisions and ultimate cost. When the risk areas have been resolved, then fixed prices might be more appropriate.

Risk analysis can also expose possible areas of conflict between the contractor and client. These can then be addressed early in the project life cycle, thus reducing the likelihood of disagreement (or even litigation) as a result of misunderstanding.

H4 *Allows a more meaningful assessment and justification of contingencies*

Many managers apply blanket contingency levels on no better basis than a 'gut feeling'. This often results in over- or underprovision and the ineffective application of scarce resources. Risk management can identify and quantify the amount of contingency required to give a particular acceptable confidence level, and the risk budget can be actively managed as the project proceeds. The overall budget for the project, and especially the contingency fund, can then be allocated to the prime areas of risk, although generally it is better for the contingency fund to be held centrally.

H5 *Discourages the acceptance of financially unsound projects*

The discipline of assessing the impact of possible risks to a project forces realism in the planning stage as risk analysis creates an early awareness of potential obstacles and opportunities. In extreme cases, risk analysis may reveal that a project cannot meet its objectives, is not feasible, or is a potential threat. In these situations the organisation can decide not to bid or to pull out before resources are heavily committed.

H6 *Contributes to the build-up of statistical information to assist in better management of future projects*

The same problems often arise on different projects within the same organisation – even in a company that has good internal communication. This is usually due to the learning curve experienced by many project staff as a result either of transfer to new projects or promotion to new levels of responsibility. Quite often, however, it is because the decision-makers set unrealistic expectations.

Formal risk analysis, together with post-project reviews, can provide a wealth of information in a form that can be used as a reference for staff and managers alike.

H7 Risk analysis enables objective comparison of alternatives

All projects contain decision points when alternative courses of action are available. Risk management allows the relative opportunities and threats to be evaluated and compared on a common basis, supporting project decision-makers. This benefit is also applicable to the bid process where trade-offs of alternative solutions can be performed.

H8 Identifies, and allocates responsibility to, the best risk owner

Risk analysis involves looking objectively at a project and examining its strengths and weaknesses. This will highlight issues which are being addressed either by nobody or more than one person. It is a common occurrence on projects for two or more people (or departments) to 'pass the buck' for a problem between them. While 'blame' is being fought over, progress is delayed, leading to knock-on impacts elsewhere on the project. Where the ownership of a problem area is ambiguous, risk management can enable each risk to be uniquely allocated.

'Soft' benefits

S1 Improves corporate experience and general communication

Improved communication has been described as the single greatest benefit of the risk management process. Risk management provides a framework for identifying and discussing project issues in a neutral, blame-free environment, with the emphasis on positive action rather than recrimination. Many previously hidden assumptions are revealed during the process, and different members of the project team will find a common language to talk about their concerns.

The routine use of risk management techniques can also have a beneficial company-wide effect because it facilitates good communications from the lowest level to the top by encouraging full feedback from projects that have failed, thus alerting the organisation to areas deserving greater attention in the future. Creating a database of risk experiences can foster greater openness on risk issues and thus enhance future project decisions.

S2 Leads to a common understanding and improved team spirit

The risk management process brings the whole project team together with a single purpose and permits team members to go beyond their own limited contribution and gain a wider view of the project. Differences in understanding are exposed and can be reconciled not in terms of an individual's or group's competence, but in terms that are task- and activity-based. Threats are seen as the common 'enemy' to be beaten, and opportunities are prizes to be won. This stimulates people to see the project's objectives as a common goal and to work together to achieve them. Winning in a challenging environment, is a powerful, motivating, team-building influence.

Risk management creates a framework for the exchange of ideas among people from different areas of the project, with complementary skills and different perceptions of the project. Across the organisation, the use of risk management encourages the exchange of information between projects, leading to the capture of 'corporate' knowledge.

Having established a common understanding of the aims and objectives of their project, the team can use the risk management process to help agree the way in which they are going to proceed on the key issues. An agreed approach to risk management allows resources to be effectively deployed to achieve the project's goals and prevents team members going in different directions.

S3 *Helps distinguish between good luck/good management and bad luck/bad management*

In most organisations, rewards such as promotion, more interesting jobs and higher levels of remuneration arise from the success of the project. It is easy for senior management to assume that the problems a project experiences are the result of bad management and that successful projects are due to good management. In reality, of course, some projects are inherently more problematic than others. An understanding of the inherent risk in a project provides a basis for assessing the project manager's effectiveness, allowing a distinction between good management/good luck and bad management/bad luck. This leads to individual behaviour being better aligned with goals at both corporate and project levels.

S4 *Helps develop the ability of staff to assess risks*

Several benefits may accrue to individuals as a result of being exposed to risk analysis on a project. The simple fact that risk analysis is being undertaken is enough to make people more aware that risks may, and do, exist in their area of influence. As a result, they tend to look out for them not only in the current circumstances, but also when making decisions for future activities. This awareness of risk therefore improves the competence of the people involved in preparing and executing plans.

Individuals may assess their own ability by predicting risks and then seeing how this preview compares with reality. A further benefit of risk management for an individual is that it allocates the responsibility for a failure in a demonstrably unbiased way, as it is an objective consideration. This means that a project manager, for instance, will not be held personally accountable for something that he or she could not have reasonably prevented.

S5 Focuses project management attention on the real and most important issues

Formal risk management can identify those uncertainties that have the potential to seriously threaten or enhance project success. Attention and effort can then be focused on these key issues, rather than being diverted on to matters which seem important but which do not significantly affect the project's objectives.

S6 Facilitates greater risk-taking, thus increasing the benefits gained

Calculated risk-taking has always been the basis of success. In the absence of formal risk management, however, the outcome is unpredictable (little more than gambling), and opportunities remain unexploited. By applying formal risk management techniques, with appropriate mitigation and fallback plans, an organisation can take greater levels of risk with lower levels of contingency thus improving the overall return on investment.

S7 Demonstrates a responsible approach to customers

Risk management can be a basis for better customer–contractor relations. The process involves analysing customer's requirements carefully and systematically, thus encouraging the contractor to bear these in mind at all times. This in turn means that all decisions taken will be aimed at satisfying these requirements. The use of risk management on a project also encourages a better judged approach to planning objectives and timescales which then benefits the overall quality of the output. Sharing this information with the customer can lead to improved understanding and stronger relationships.

The use of an independent, objective and unbiased risk assessment process adds weight to the decisions made by the project team, and provides the customer and senior management with measures of confidence in the way the project is managed. Because risk analysis considers all aspects of a project, it will give an integrated view of a task. It generates a log of risk features against which future progress is measured and favours logical decisions to which people of various disciplines have contributed.

S8 Provides a fresh view of the personnel issues in a project

Risk management can help senior management make informed decisions about appointing project managers. For instance, it would make sense to appoint a less experienced project manager to a less risky project and vice versa.

For more senior management, risk analysis reveals those areas of a project which the project manager might otherwise choose not to expose. By being required to quantify and justify decisions, project managers are discouraged from clouding them in mystique. This helps break down any power struggle between senior and project management for the benefit of the project's objectives.

Independent risk analysis can draw attention to areas of dispute between colleagues. It can also be used to review the disposition of staff on a project in the light of the priorities it uncovers. An independent analyst can bring all the unspoken rules and motivations into the open, helping to eliminate bias. It will reveal and serve to reconcile differing perceptions of the uncertainties at hand.

THE RELATIVE MERIT OF HARD AND SOFT BENEFITS

The 'hard' and 'soft' benefits gained from implementing risk management on a project can be summarised as follows.

- It provides data to support the planning and decision-making processes.
- It helps focus the way in which the project team thinks, behaves and works together.

Without in any way minimising the benefits of the first of these, it is quite probably the second that has the greater impact. Many experienced risk practitioners will argue that a proportion of the benefits of the risk process are achieved in the activities leading up to the first risk register, long before any risk-mitigating action has been taken. This is because the whole project team will have appreciated the issues and will be aware of their own contribution and know what they need to do for best effect. This legacy of understanding will remain with the team throughout the project. Ongoing risk monitoring and reporting also reinforces the acceptance of responsibility, thus ensuring that an appropriate proportion of available energy is expended in managing the risk.

BENEFITS FROM DIFFERENT PERSPECTIVES WITHIN THE ORGANISATION

The benefits listed above were primarily focused at the project manager level within the organisation. However, other levels within the organisation are likely to have a different perspective on the benefits. Table 2.2 identifies some examples at the corporate and individual levels.

'Hard' benefits

H9 Compliance with corporate governance requirements

Projects are not only a significant contributor to the organisation's progress and the generation of shareholder value, they can also be a significant source of threat to the organisation. Recognised best practice in corporate

Table 2.2 *The 'hard' and 'soft' benefits of project risk management throughout the organisation*

'Hard' Benefits	'Soft' Benefits
H9 Compliance with corporate governance requirements	S9 Better reputation as a result of fewer headline project failures
H10 A greater potential for future business with existing customers	S10 Better customer relations due to improved performance on current projects
H11 Reduced cost base	S11 A less stressful working environment

governance (such as Turnbull in the UK and Sarbanes-Oxley in the US) requires that organisations have a formal system for recognising, evaluating, managing and escalating threats arising from activities undertaken both within and outside the organisation. Risk management in projects is clearly an important element of fulfilling this requirement.

H10 A greater potential for future business with existing customers

The achievement of objectives on current projects often leads directly to follow-on business or preferred supplier status with existing customers as trust and confidence increases.

H11 Reduced cost base

Clear quantification of the impact of threats and the potential of opportunities leads to the elimination of hidden contingencies and the proper factoring of contingency over the portfolio of risk. This often produces a lower, but realistic, cost base that is still sufficiently robust to cope with the cost impact of uncertainties in the project.

'Soft' benefits

S9 Better reputation as a result of fewer headline project failures

Reputation is difficult to quantify but vital in maintaining an organisation's trading position and brand value. It is established and enhanced by building a track record of successful project delivery. Conversely, the failure of high-profile projects can cause severe, and often lasting, damage to reputation.

S10 Better customer relations due to improved performance on current projects

A customer's perception of good and improving performance and their observation of the application of effective risk management generally leads to improved sharing of information, more open relationships and a greater sense of partnership.

S11 A less stressful project environment

Management by crisis becomes wearing on all project participants, leading to poor decision-making, absenteeism and loss of key skills. Risk management reduces these stresses by enabling not only the planning of fallback activities before a foreseeable crisis arises, but also the execution of proactive steps to prevent or reduce the impact of the crisis in advance and to improve the likelihood and benefit of opportunities.

THREATS TO EFFECTIVE RISK MANAGEMENT PROCESSES

It would be easy to conclude that implementing risk management is always a positive activity and that the process will necessarily create a cohesive and synergistic team all by itself. However, there are potential dangers in applying the process which can give rise to negative responses and, at least as importantly, can also lead to bad project decisions about risk situations. The following list contains some of the more common issues with, and objections to, the risk management process.

Risk analysis can be garbage in, gospel out

First, the results of the risk process are only as good as the information supplied. Risk practitioners must be careful to verify the input information and to identify and eliminate bias as far as possible. Project objectives should be clearly defined, and the assumptions recorded and agreed.

In addition, the project risk management process should be explicit about testing the consistency of the expert judgements of those involved in order to make the best possible decisions.

Second, output from the formal risk process still has to be evaluated and interpreted. There is danger that results will be accepted uncritically, leading to decisions being made without a real understanding of the underlying issues.

But, don't forget NINO – Nothing In, Nothing Out. Something has to be done!

Ownership may be transferred to the risk facilitator or risk process owner

The application of risk techniques often involves using specialist staff with particular expertise, either in-house or external consultants. This introduces the danger of viewing risk as the responsibility of the risk specialists rather than as an integral part of the project management task. The risk process must be owned by the project team, and the results used by them to modify project strategy where appropriate.

The validity of risk analysis can become stale

An assessment of risk exposure is merely a snapshot of the project at the time of the assessment. Circumstances change rapidly in most projects, and the results and recommendations of the risk process have a limited lifetime. This means that the risk report will quickly become out-of-date, and its recommendations must be quickly acted upon if they are to be effective. Yet it is not unusual to find projects that are still using the original assessment of risks many months or years later. The risk register should be a live document that is updated on a frequent basis, not just for important risk review meetings.

The effectiveness of the risk management process is difficult to prove

It is difficult to measure and demonstrate the effectiveness of the overall risk management process since it deals with issues that are intrinsically uncertain. If risks that were identified fail to materialise, was that due to good risk management or poor risk identification? If a project is completed under budget, how much of the underspend can be attributed to the results of the risk reduction measures and what proportion was due to high initial estimating? These are questions that risk practitioners grapple with as they try to quantify their contribution to project success.

The process can antagonise staff

If people within the team are not committed to the risk management process there is a danger that the risk practitioner may 'oversell' the benefits without balancing these downside issues. This may lead to a lack of credibility in the process and could demotivate staff. This problem could equally well arise with project staff or senior management – wherever there is a lack of flexibility and willingness to embrace new ideas.

Benefits to timescale and budget is not achieved

Often, risk management will be introduced into a project team, but only a 'tick in the box' result will be achieved. The project will have a risk process, a risk register, a risk analysis, risk mitigation plans and risk reports, but the team stops short of carrying out the most important step of the process – carrying out the actions to mitigate the risks proactively. This will result in the highly desirable improvements to timescale and cost being lost.

CONCLUSION

There are significant benefits to be gained within the project and throughout the organisation from the application of risk management. Whilst some of these benefits are not readily quantifiable, they can be significant in improving reputation, confidence and performance from the personal to the corporate level. A clear understanding of the objectives of the process and communication of the role to be played by each member of the team will help ensure that resources expended on risk management provide a good return on investment.

3

Principles

This chapter sets out the key principles of risk management as embodied in the *PRAM Guide*, and puts them in the context of a summary of the recommended risk management process (expanded in Chapter 4), laying the foundation for the detailed chapters which follow.

TERMINOLOGY

Terminology in the risk management field is varied and often confused, and clear definition of terms is therefore required. The definitions used in this *Guide* are presented in the Glossary, but two particular definitions are highlighted here as they are essential to a proper understanding of the remainder of the *Guide*.

The word 'risk' can be interpreted in many ways. In this *Guide* two distinctly different uses are recognised.

- The term 'risk event' describes an individual uncertainty which can be identified, assessed and managed through the project risk management process, and is defined as follows: 'A risk event is an uncertain event or set of circumstances that, should it occur, will have an effect on achievement of one or more of the project's objectives.'
- The term 'project risk' is used to describe the joint effect of risk events and other sources of uncertainty. At an overall project level, project risk, rather than individual risk events must be the focus, but it is important to understand how project risk is defined by its components, and to manage it at both levels. Project risk is defined as follows: 'Project risk is the exposure of stakeholders to the consequences of variations in outcome.'

Project risk therefore results largely from the accumulation of a number of individual risk events, together with other sources of uncertainty to the project as a whole, such as variability and ambiguity.

17

A key principle in the definition of risk event used in this *Guide* is the recognition that uncertainty can affect the achievement of a project's objectives either positively or negatively. The term 'risk event' is therefore used to cover both uncertainties that could hinder the project (threats) and uncertainties that could help the project (opportunities). As a result, the risk management process is designed to avoid and minimise threats as well as to exploit and maximise opportunities. The aim of addressing both types of uncertainty in the single risk management process is to optimise achievement of project objectives.

THE RISK MANAGEMENT PROCESS

The risk management process recommended in this *Guide* comprises a number of phases. These are summarised in this chapter, and discussed in more detail in Chapter 4. Each phase is a required element of the process, although they can be implemented at different levels of detail. Some phases can be divided into sub-phases if a more complex process is required, or implemented as a single phase for simple projects. The chosen level of process detail should be determined by the specific requirements of the individual project.

The level of risk management process implementation may depend on the degree of maturity of organisational risk management capability. Those organisations with broad experience of applying risk management to their business and projects are likely to be more comfortable implementing a more complex risk management process where this is required or justified, whereas organisations at lower levels of risk management maturity will typically prefer a simpler process for most projects. There is, however, an irreducible minimum process level below which risk management will be ineffective. An assessment of organisational risk management maturity may assist an organisation in understanding how to improve risk management effectiveness, and may form the basis for development of improved capability.

The simplest description of the risk management process has five phases, as shown in Figure 3.1, together with a 'Manage Process' activity. These can be elaborated into sub-phases as described below.

The risk management process is iterative within itself, so the output from each phase might require a previous phase to be revisited. In Figure 3.1 the thicker solid lines indicates the major iterative loop, thinner solid lines show other possible links back to earlier phases, and the dotted lines represent the requirement to manage the process at all stages.

In addition to the internal loops, the entire risk management process must be repeated throughout the project life cycle. The first iteration should be conducted at a strategic level to indicate those areas requiring further, more detailed, attention. Ideally, this would be performed prior to

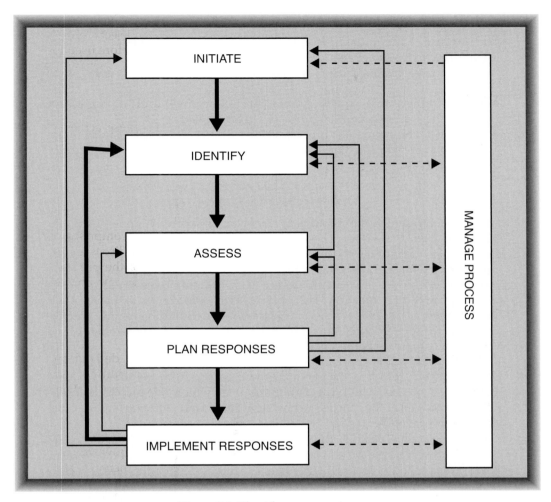

Figure 3.1 *The risk management process*

project initiation, when key decisions can be informed by the outcome of the risk process. Subsequent iterations might be undertaken at key points in the project life cycle or at regular intervals, with the frequency determined by the specific requirements of the project. A different level of risk management process may be appropriate at different stages of the project life cycle.

The risk management process must be fully integrated with other project management processes. Risk information must be used to inform other parts of the project process, including project planning, estimating, resource planning, change management, quality management and stakeholder management.

Initiate

The purpose of the Initiate phase is to set the scope, objectives and context for the risk management process. This phase may be further divided into two sub-phases: Define Project, and Focus Risk Management Process:

- **Define Project** aims to ensure common understanding of the project to which the risk management process is to be applied.
- **Focus Risk Management Process** fits the details of the risk management process to the specific requirements of the project.

Define Project

Any project to which the risk management process is to be applied should have *well-defined objectives*. These should reflect the interests of all project stakeholders, including those commissioning the project, and should be supported by measurable criteria for success. Where there is more than one project objective, the relative importance of each should be defined.

Any project to which the risk management process is to be applied should have a *well-defined scope*. The scope definition should specify precisely what constitutes the project: what is included and excluded; by whom the project is being conducted; and how the project may relate to other projects being conducted by other parties. The scope should be defined in such terms as the products to be output from the project or the activities to be conducted, the timeframe over which the project is to be implemented and the parties whose products and activities are to be considered part of the project.

Any project to which the risk management process is to be applied should have a *well-defined strategy* and an *outline plan* for the execution of the project. Both of these should be sufficiently defined and understood to enable a risk strategy to be tailored to the specific needs of the project.

Should the project lack adequate definition of objectives, scope, strategy or plan, this shortfall needs to be rectified before the risk management process as described here can proceed effectively. Any shortfall can be addressed by applying the risk management process at a strategic level.

Focus Risk Management Process

The objectives of the risk management process should be well understood and documented prior to its application to a project. They should be defined with reference to the objectives of the project concerned, as well as any higher-level requirements such as strategic risk management or corporate governance processes. The defined objectives of each particular application of the risk management process should be reviewed periodically throughout implementation, and updated appropriately.

The risk management process should be applied immediately at the outset of the project (ideally before significant commitments are made) and should continue in an appropriate form throughout the project life cycle.

The project risk management strategy should also be established at the outset of the project. Due consideration should be given to the risk management objectives and policy, procedures, methods, organisation, roles and the infrastructure of staff, skills and tools. The decisions made about the risk management strategy should be adequately documented (typically as a risk management plan). Responsibility for ensuring that a project has adequate risk management measures in place, and that these are applied in practice, rests with the project manager.

The depth or level at which the risk management process should be applied at each stage of the project life cycle should be commensurate with project circumstances. The factors to be considered in determining an appropriate level of intensity should include:

- the importance of the project to the organisation conducting it
- project size or value
- project complexity
- the degree to which the project represents change
- the perceived stability of the project baseline
- the novelty of the approach that is planned
- any prior knowledge of the level of project risk faced.

These factors may change as a result of project progress, so the intensity of the risk management process should be adjusted accordingly.

The roles to be played by project team members in implementing the risk management process should be well defined, adequately tasked and the compliance of their performance assured. Part of these roles will include taking responsibility for responses to specific risk events. The aim should be to gain the commitment of the individuals concerned, while putting in place adequate control processes to assure their performance.

The project risk management process should be appropriately interfaced with any risk management process conducted by other interested parties. It should be noted that some types of project risk or risk events are more amenable to successful control through a cooperative effort. Others may be commercially sensitive or external to the project or the organisation, and therefore require different management arrangements.

For a continuing project, the risk management process should be applied on a cyclical basis, so that the assessment of project risk exposure may be kept up-to-date and the project's response adjusted as necessary. The times at which the elements of the risk management process are applied should be determined in line with the needs of the real-time environment within which the project is to be progressed and the intensity of risk management process which the project justifies.

When an important decision has to be made with regard to a project or a prospective project (such as a bid), risk management principles should be used to establish a 'snapshot' of the level of project risk and its implications at that time, which may or may not lead to a cyclical process.

The risk management process should be conducted as an integral part of the project management process. This issue should be addressed at a cultural, as well as a management, level within the organisation. The organisation structure installed to support the project's risk management process should form an integral part of the project management team, not a 'bolt-on extra', but with the benefit of expert support from outside the project where this may be deemed necessary.

Adequate resources should be provided for the effective practice of the risk management process, at the appropriate depth and intensity that the project justifies.

The project's requirement for risk-related information and data should be well defined and proper arrangements made for its provision. The information and data should be adequate to fulfil the risk management principles specified, again at the intensity of the risk management process that the project justifies.

Records should be kept of a project's use of risk management, consistent with the overall project information processes, and adequate for the purpose of implementing and managing the risk management process. The information should be recorded in a form that promotes the efficiency of the risk management process and should offer an audit trail. The records should be suitable for the purpose of the project learning from its own history. Where appropriate, records may also be kept so as to enable the lessons learned from a project to be applied to the organisation's future projects.

Finally, proper application of a project's nominated risk management procedures should be assured through the QA system, including provision for audit.

Identify

The purpose of the Identify phase is to enable the risk events relevant to a project to be identified as comprehensively as is possible, practical and cost-effective. The options for risk response for some risk events may also naturally be identified during this phase. If not identified now, they must clearly be identified later as part of the Plan Responses phase.

An approach should be adopted to risk identification that gives confidence in the project's ability to compile a list of risk events which is as complete as possible, embracing all relevant types and sources of risk event. Stakeholders should be consulted, and external opinions should be sought where appropriate and practical. Relevant lessons should be learned from the risk management experience of earlier, comparable projects, to which those conducting the current project may have access.

The aim should be to elicit reasonably objective information and the method used should promote an open response from the individuals who may be approached.

After a risk event has been identified, it should be validated as far as possible in terms of both the truth of the initial information about the risk event and the accuracy of the description initially built up of the risk event's characteristics. The amount of effort put into validation should be commensurate with the likelihood or otherwise that data gathered about the risk event may be inaccurate.

Assess

The Assess phase aims to increase the understanding of each identified risk event to a level where appropriate and effective decisions can be taken. In addition to considering individual risk events, the level of overall project risk should also be assessed. The assessment of individual risk events and of the combined effect of risks on the project may be undertaken using a qualitative and/or a quantitative approach as appropriate to the project's circumstances. This Assess phase can involve a number of sub-phases (Structure, Ownership, Estimate, Evaluate), or can be undertaken as a single step. Details of the sub-phases are given in Chapter 4.

The information assembled about each risk event should describe all relevant characteristics, including the nature of the uncertainty faced and the nature of its (positive or negative) potential for impact on project objectives.

As far as is practical, assessments should be made of a risk event's probability of occurrence and potential impact. Other information can be included where appropriate. The relative significance of each of the risk events identified should be assessed in terms of the level of threat posed to the achievement of the project's objectives or the opportunity to enhance their achievement. Using a risk impact window – an indication of when the impact is likely to occur – can also help in prioritising risk events. This can be linked to the project plan, ensuring adequate time to address each risk event proactively. As well as the individual potential effect of each risk event, there may be additional effects from a combination of risk events. The combined effect of all the identified risk events should be assessed, possibly using a simulation modelling approach.

Where preliminary responses have been identified, their likely effectiveness and their cost implications should be determined. Where responses have not yet been identified, the assessment (whether qualitative or quantitative) should be regarded as preliminary and should be revisited once the Plan Responses phase has been completed (see the next section), in order to take account of agreed responses and evaluate their likely effectiveness.

The Assess phase should be viewed as giving a 'snapshot' of project risk exposure at a point in time, allowing for the plans made for the project, the current status of the risk events and the effectiveness of risk responses in place at that time.

This assessment should be used as an input to the decisions to be made regarding the prioritisation of risk responses. It should take due account of the timing of impacts of risk events and of any interdependencies there may be among risk events and their effects.

Plan Responses

The Plan Responses phase exists to determine appropriate responses to individual risk events and to ensure that the assessment of the level of overall project risk is used to set or modify project strategy. These two aims can be addressed through two sub-phases, Plan Risk Event Responses and Plan Project Risk Responses, or they may be addressed together.

Plan Responses will result in an iteration of the risk management process. Plan Risk Event Responses feeds back to the Identify and Assess phases, since acting on risk responses will affect identified risk events and may result in emergent risk events as well as secondary risk events. Plan Project Risk Responses feeds back to the Initiate phase, as the level of overall project risk may require changes to the project strategy or to the whole risk management process.

Plan Risk Event Responses

Risk responses to identified individual risk events should be developed and implemented as appropriate, justifiable and practical. The aim is to avoid or minimise threats, and to exploit or maximise opportunities, in order to optimise the likelihood of achieving project objectives.

This sub-phase should start by considering any preliminary responses already identified during the Identify phase; these responses should now be re-evaluated and new responses identified if they are no longer appropriate. All other risk events for which responses have not previously been identified must be reviewed during this phase, and appropriate responses developed.

There is typically a trade-off between the resources committed to risk responses and the effect on achieving the project objectives. Risk response action should be taken only when the project manager is convinced that the response is efficient in terms of the expected gain in achievement of the project objectives. Where practical, sensitivity analysis and/or trade-off studies should be applied in making decisions about risk responses. In determining whether a response is justified, the project manager should take into account:

- the relative importance of the various project objectives
- the significance of the risk event concerned, relative to the project objectives
- the potential effectiveness of the response in addressing the risk event and hence in enabling achievement of the project objectives
- the likely effect on project timescale, budget and performance

- the expected cost of taking the action (including opportunity cost), compared with possible later costs if the action were not taken and the risk event occurs (if a threat) or is missed (if an opportunity)
- the possibility of introducing secondary risk events into the project as a result of implementing the response action
- the availability of resources for risk response action.

Where risk response development includes fallback planning, there should be well-defined trigger conditions for taking action. To ensure that it is apparent when the trigger conditions occur, it is essential to have an effective process for monitoring project progress.

Having developed appropriate responses, the risk management process should iterate back to the Assess phase to reassess the risk events in the light of agreed responses.

Project plans should include a level of contingency commensurate with the scale of overall project risk faced and to the level required for an acceptable probability of project success (or confidence level).

Plan Project Risk Responses

This sub-phase uses the insights provided by earlier phases to improve project implementation. This will include taking account of overall project risk in project planning and risk management planning.

Plan Project Risk Responses iterates back to the Initiate phase of the risk management process, as well as affecting overall project strategy. The first iteration of the risk management process is likely to be at a strategic high level, and the results from this must be used to inform the ongoing conduct of the project and later iterations of its risk management process.

The key principle is the need to use a reasonably strategic level of planning to manage project risk effectively and efficiently early in the project, developing the detail necessary to implement the project based on the first pass through the risk management process. Separating Plan Project Risk Responses in this way saves unnecessary detailed planning time and effort for the project and avoids the severe limitations which arise if risk management is attempted at a detailed tactical level without prior strategic analysis. This is critical for all projects, regardless of size or complexity. The key deliverable is an effective project plan which incorporates the results from earlier risk management phases.

Implement Responses

The Implement Responses phase ensures that effective actions are taken based on the decisions made during the Plan Responses phase. This includes both actions to implement risk responses targeting individual risk events and actions affecting the overall strategic planning and direction of the project based on assessment of project risk.

Responsibilities for implementing the planned risk responses should be well defined and unambiguously allocated to nominated individuals. Responses should be verifiable and response owners should be accountable for the outcome. Individuals charged with executing risk responses for specific risk events should be empowered with appropriate information, authority and resources – in the same way as for other project management tasks.

The developing circumstances of each risk event should be monitored so that the risk response and/or contingency may be adjusted or acted on appropriately. This should involve re-applying the approach described in the earlier phases to the situation as it changes. Well-defined close-out criteria should be established to determine at which point each risk event can be removed from the attention of the risk management process.

Project stakeholders should be provided with current and accurate risk information at a level and frequency appropriate to their interests and needs. For example, risk response owners should receive detailed information on the specific risk events for which they are required to take action; the project manager needs information on all risk events facing the project, including priorities, resource implications, timing and so on; and those responsible for making decisions about the project's strategic direction should receive information about the level of overall project risk to enable strategic decision-making. Risk information should be provided in a range of risk reports, covering such aspects as the nature of the individual risk events, the combined effect of their impact on project objectives, priorities for risk reduction, the status of risk reduction and contingency provision. The project strategy and plan should be evolved in line with the decisions made about risk responses and with changes in overall project risk.

The Implement Responses phase should also address the effectiveness of the risk management process, determining whether it fulfils the scope and objectives set during the Initiate phase. Process modifications should be made where necessary, and documented in the risk management plan.

Manage Process

The Manage Process activity exists to ensure that the risk management process remains effective in addressing identified risk events and project risk. It takes input from each phase of the risk management process and reviews the approach adopted for each phase, as well as for the process as a whole. This activity covers every aspect of implementing the risk management process, including tools and techniques, intensity of implementation, roles and responsibilities, communication and reporting requirements and so on. It also covers the integration of the risk management process with other project management and business processes.

This activity is the responsibility of the project manager, who must ensure that the risk management process, as applied to the project, is fully effective at all times in addressing the level of risk faced by the project, both in terms of individual identified risk events and the overall level of project risk. Effectiveness is defined in terms of resource usage, extent to which the process is proactive rather than reactive, timeliness of responses and so on.

The Manage Process activity might be performed through formal and regular risk management process reviews, or may be conducted informally throughout the project.

CONCLUSION

This chapter has introduced the key principles of risk management which are further developed in the remainder of the *PRAM Guide*, including definition of the key terms 'risk event' and 'project risk', and an outline of the recommended risk management process. Chapter 4 provides a fuller description of the risk management process and indicates how it might be applied at both strategic and tactical levels within a project.

4

The PRAM process

This chapter explains why a risk management process is important, the main features of the PRAM 1997 process and some key developments and changes for the PRAM 2004 process.

INTRODUCTION

In this chapter we will describe the PRAM process in generic terms, using the phase and sub-phase structure provided in Chapter 3 and summarised in Figure 4.1.

A process is a road map for formalising planning. Metaphorically speaking, a good generic process is a set of maps covering all possible journeys, with guidance on how to select the map and then the route appropriate for a particular trip. Good maps, and the ability to use them effectively, are vital in unknown territory, and they remain useful until the territory involved is understood in the same way by everyone concerned with planning a journey.

Table 4.1 shows how PRAM 2004 has improved on, and developed from, PRAM 1997. Some of the points in the table may seem complicated to first-time users of project risk management processes. However, a key feature of PRAM 2004 is that it facilitates movement from a simple starting position and process to the most effective best-practice processes. It is important to understand, at least in outline, what best practice looks like before introducing project risk management or improving existing practices. The process itself must facilitate learning, moving from current practice towards better practice, which PRAM 2004 is designed to do in a more focused way than PRAM 1997.

A HYPOTHETICAL SITUATION FOR INITIAL DISCUSSION

As Chapter 3 indicated, it is important to initiate a project risk management process as early as possible in the project life cycle and apply the process regularly as the project evolves, adjusting it to suit the project's life-cycle

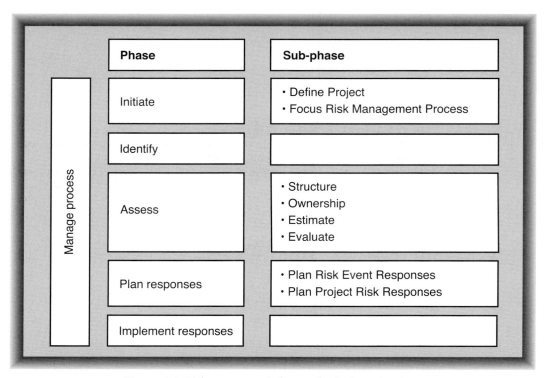

Figure 4.1 *Risk management phase and sub-phase structure*

position at each application. To describe the process in any detail there needs to be clarity as to which stage is being discussed. For present purposes a five-stage project life cycle, as detailed in section 5 of BS 6079–1, will be used:

1 **Conception** – covering the period from the emergence of an idea for a project to an initial formal statement of a user's or sponsor's needs
2 **Feasibility** – establishing both the technical and commercial viability of the project
3 **Implementation** – undertaking the project
4 **Operation** – using deliverables from the project for their intended purposes
5 **Termination** – closing down the project.

Organisations commonly introduce a project risk management process towards the end of the feasibility stage, and this is also the easiest point at which to explain what is involved. Hence, it is assumed that the project is approaching the end of the feasibility stage, with well developed strategic plans, and is about to seek sanction to proceed.

Two other issues are best dealt with by assuming a particular situation. First, the extent and the nature of previous applications of risk management processes should influence subsequent applications. Second, a contractor can

Table 4.1 *Comparison of process between PRAM 1997 and PRAM 2004*

	PRAM 1997	**PRAM 2004**
Initiate phase	Most project risk management processes have an Initiate phase, that part of the process concerned with getting started. A unique feature of the PRAM Initiate phase is the guidance provided (in the Focus sub-phase) on how to adapt the generic process to the project of immediate concern, choosing the best map for the purpose in hand and reading it effectively.	
Identify phase	Most risk management processes start the analysis proper with an Identify phase, concerned with identification of sources of uncertainty that threats. Some also consider opportunities. A key feature of PRAM is the effective linkage of threats and opportunities to responses specific to particular issues plus 'general' responses which deal with sets of issues and build in the flexibility to deal with unanticipated threats and opportunities.	This linkage has been further developed in this edition, by adopting a second definition of risk ('project risk' as well as 'risk events'), which facilitates a search for 'best' approaches to a project, as distinct from just 'good enough'.
Assess phase	Most approaches to project risk management have an Assess phase involving qualitative (PI matrix) and quantitative (probabilistic) estimation. PRAM does this in a way which allows the overall process shape to reflect a focus on either a qualitative or quantitative estimation, or an intermediate position. In particular, if the focus is entry-level analysis based on a PI approach, it is natural and normal to consider response generation after an Assess phase, but if the focus is effective probabilistic analysis, the sequence has to be reversed. In the context of an iterative process the sequence matters less, but it still matters.	A key feature of PRAM is its iterative nature. One-pass processes are inherently inefficient, because some issues receive too much attention, and others not enough. The aim of an iterative process is to apply 80 per cent of time to the 20 per cent of the issues that matter most. The feedback loop structure discussion in this edition has been further developed to clarify what is involved.
Plan phase	This is concerned with detailed planning for implementation after initial use of the PRAM process at a strategic planning level.	This edition gives separate consideration to these two very different planning issues within the Plan phase, emphasising the difference between specific and general response planning and thus dealing with specific risk events and overall project risk.
Manage phase [PRAM 2004– Implement]	This is concerned with managing both risk in the project and the risk process itself.	This edition considers these different aspects of management by specifying a Manage Process activity to embody the management of the process and an Implement Responses phase to emphasise the need to ensure that the planned responses are carried out.

avoid accepting risk events in the first place, or pass them on to subcontractors. A client may wish to pass risk events on, but a client ultimately owns all risk not transferred effectively, and client versions of risk management must reflect this position. In this chapter, the client perspective has been taken.

The iterative (multiple-pass looping) structure of risk management processes can either be complex and potentially confusing or simplistic and ineffective. Figure 4.2 illustrates this iterative structure by way of a Gantt chart, and, in practice, it can be very useful to plan a project risk management process in this manner. However, it would not normally be worth showing the detail associated with the second and third complete cycles.

There is nothing magic about using three iterations, but three is a reasonable target. One is invariably too few; five is usually too many. A useful related rule of thumb is to try to finish the first iteration in about 20 per cent of the time available. This is a version of the 80:20 rule – try to spend about 80 per cent of your time on the 20 per cent that matters most. The proportion might vary depending on the context.

In Figure 4.2 strategic-level risk management refers to that period during which the activities of the Conception and Feasibility stages of the five-stage project life cycle of BS 6079–1 would typically be undertaken. Tactical-level risk management covers the remaining stages.

AN EXAMPLE: FIRST COMPLETE CYCLE OF STRATEGIC-LEVEL RISK MANAGEMENT

Initiate

A first pass through the **Initiate–Define Project** sub-phase should be as complete as possible. The purpose of this sub-phase is to consolidate relevant information about the project in a form suitable as a basis for risk management at this stage in the project life cycle, filling in any gaps that are revealed. All the analysis that follows is built on the foundation provided by this sub-phase, and it is obviously best if this is as sound as possible. However, some gaps and inconsistencies will usually be identified that cannot be resolved immediately, and these will need to be worked round in the meantime.

It can be useful to approach this sub-phase in terms of seeking answers to seven questions about the project:

1	Who are the parties involved?	(parties)
2	What do the parties involved want to achieve?	(objectives)
3	What is it that the parties are interested in?	(design)
4	How is it to be done?	(activities)
5	What resources are required?	(resources)
6	When does it have to be done?	(timetable)
7	What does the rest of the project life cycle look like?	(life cycle)

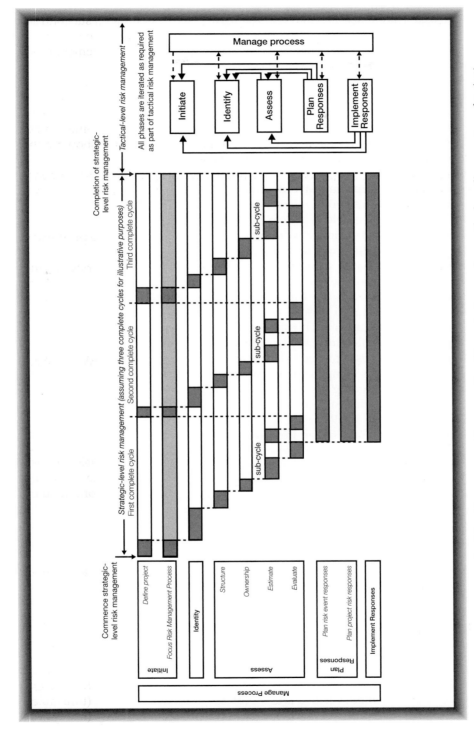

Figure 4.2 *An example of the risk management focus over time (timescale: days, weeks, months depending on nature of project)*

If an organisation has a low level of maturity in terms of project risk management, it may be inclined to focus on activities as the key source of risk. But it is important to appreciate that a failure on the part of the project owner to articulate objectives clearly is a major source of risk, as is a failure to align objectives for all the key parties, to link these objectives to a well-defined strategy, and to link this strategy to strategic plans in terms of cash flow, design, activity and resource requirements. Each party is likely to have multiple objectives – the classic cost–time–quality triad for example – and appropriate trade-offs need to be understood. For instance, if a risk event occurs that results in delay, the choice may be between buying the lost time or lowering quality expectations. The decision made will depend on the client's view of appropriate trade-offs, as well as on the implications of the available response options.

The target deliverable is a clear, unambiguous, shared understanding of all key aspects of the project within an appropriate scope of analysis that is documented, verified and reported. This target may not be reached on the first pass, but what is achieved on each subsequent pass must be 'fit for purpose' in terms of the rest of that pass.

A first pass through the **Initiate–Focus Risk Management Process** sub-phase can take place in parallel with the Define Project sub-phase first pass, as indicated in Figure 4.2. The purpose of this sub-phase is to prepare strategic plans and detailed tactical plans for the project risk management process, shaping generic best practice to the needs of this particular application. Such plans should be as complete as possible before the rest of the first pass gets underway, but ongoing development and revisions as the first pass continues should be anticipated, as indicated by the lower-level activity (lighter shading) in Figure 4.2. Prior to exploring the risk associated with a particular project there is usually uncertainty about the nature and severity of that risk.

It can be useful to view the project risk management process as a whole, as a programme (portfolio of related projects), and all sub-phases as projects within the programme portrayed by Figure 4.2. Hence, best-practice project management, including project risk management, applies to the higher-order 'planning the planning' involved here. For example, if the project risk management process is being carried out by the client's team, questions which need to be answered include:

- What does the client want to achieve via the project risk management process?
- Will the selected project risk management process design deliver what is wanted?
- What resources are required for the project risk management process?
- When is delivery of results required?

The deliverable for this sub-phase phase is a clear, unambiguous, shared understanding of all relevant key aspects of the project risk management process, documented, verified and reported. All these key aspects must be fit for purpose in relation to each pass.

Identify

A first pass through the **Identify** phase might involve identifying key risk events and obvious associated responses. Both threats and opportunities are relevant. A simple residual risk event with a label like 'normal productivity variations' is useful as a collection device for risk events that are not worth separate, exhaustive identification, and will ensure that nothing is left out. For some activities, this residual category may be all that is needed, with some illustrative examples. In terms of time risk this amounts to assuming that a basic PERT (program evaluation and review technique) model may be appropriate, given examples of relevant risk events. The activity structure from the Define Project sub-phase should be used to identify risk events, one activity at a time, with the other six questions addressed in the Initiate–Define Project sub-phase providing a structure for further identification. In other words, design components and their integration are sources of risk events, as are resource issues, contracting issues and so on. At least one response needs to be identified for each risk event to consider the impact later in this cycle, but a positive decision to 'do nothing for now' may be appropriate for most risk events on the first pass of risk identification. A first pass at compiling the risk log or register is the output of this phase, with a start on associated response analysis.

Assess

A first pass through the **Assess–Structure** sub-phase might involve testing the structure used so far for robustness and a sensible level of detail. For example, are two risk events so closely related in terms of the same response that treating them as a single risk would be satisfactory? Or does one risk event actually involve two quite different sets of possible issues which implies that it might more usefully be treated as two separate risk events?

A first pass through the **Assess–Ownership** sub-phase is usefully focused on being clear, in strategic terms, which risks the client proposes to own and manage and which risks contractors are expected to own and manage. This may be a matter of corporate policy for all projects, but some organisations may consider it on a project-by-project basis, and special cases may be specific to particular aspects of projects in organisations with a mature risk management culture.

A first pass through the **Assess–Estimate** sub-phase must address each of the risk events identified earlier. The first issue is whether the risk event in question can be usefully directly associated with a quantifying process, or whether it is better handled as an assumption or condition, which may need some form of collective sizing later. For example, if the project is building housing to let, 'ground conditions better or worse than expected' may be an opportunity and threat worth quantifying, but 'major archaeology find', whose effects would be catastrophic and difficult to define, may be a risk event best identified and managed without attempting measurement if it is deemed very unlikely. In general it is not useful to attempt quantification of 'force majeure' risks of this kind for project duration planning purposes, but they must not be overlooked in business case assessments. For those risk events worth quantifying, several alternative approaches are commonly recognised.

One approach is direct quantification using probability distribution shapes assumed appropriate to the context, like a Beta distribution approximation for activity durations as advocated for the original PERT models, or a negative exponential distribution for the interval between random failures. It is illustrated in the Appendix in Figure A.11.

A second approach is based on probability-impact (P-I) matrices. This approach is often deemed useful when good data is not available, objective probabilities are not feasible, and it is thought more appropriate in such cases to decide whether a risk event has a high, medium or low probability and a high, medium or low impact. A tick in a box in a P-I matrix provides this classification. The boundaries of the boxes can be simply defined – for example, 'medium probability' means 0.2 to 0.8 and 'medium impact' means £10 000 to £100 000. Sometimes a risk index (P-I score) is used – a single parameter metric for risk based on an assessment of the probability and impact of the risk. This approach is described in the Appendix at A2.3 under the heading, probability-impact scores.

A third approach is a 'minimalist' quantitative approach. In effect, subjective probabilities are embraced directly from a decision analysis perspective. In the P-I matrix example above, the probability could be assumed to be uniformly distributed between 0.2 and 0.8, and the impact could be assumed to be uniformly distributed between £10 000 and £100 000. However, each risk event can have such a P-I matrix box defined for it, in terms of a minimum and maximum plausible probability and impact. There is no need for a common box structure, but more importantly, there is also no need for a single parameter risk measure which fails to discriminate between expected outcomes and project risk. This approach is discussed in the Appendix at A3.2.

The first pass through the **Assess–Evaluate** sub-phase is about combining the uncertainty associated with individual risk events and deciding what to do about the implications. It is about helping us to make choices with respect to both managing project risk and the risk management process. It is important to do this a little at a time, in order to understand the relative importance of each contribution to overall uncertainty and project risk, how different sources of uncertainty fit together, and the role of statistical dependence. How the mechanics of the combination procedure works will depend on the approach adopted in the Identify-Estimate sub-phase. Whichever approach is used, a structuring of the combination sequence to reflect categories of risk and dependence structures is important. To continue our housing project example, all the ground work and foundation risk events might be grouped together, as might the structure fabrication risk events and so on, with separate groups related to revenue issues (occupancy rates and rent levels), planning issues and the like.

Direct quantitative approaches have well-established procedures to combine probability distributions, usually based on Monte Carlo sampling methods (see the Appendix at A3.3). If these methods are used, diagrams like Figure 4.3 can be used to depict the size of each contribution relative to the overall result, as a basis for understanding what matters and associated process choices.

In Figure 4.3 the impact of six issues have been modelled. Each issue has produced its own probability curve which are combined to give a cumulative effect – that is, curve 3 shows the result of issues 1+2+3. Issue 5 has the greatest impact on the project, indicated by the widest gap between the curves, and issue 3 the least. This means that using the Estimate–Evaluate sub-loop to refine the estimation of issue 5, and then revisiting all aspects of its management via a complete Define Project–Evaluate loop, would seem to be time well spent. It also means that further effort expended on issue 3 would be a low priority. Figure 4.3 demonstrates how useful Monte Carlo sampling methods can be when the results are displayed in a format that

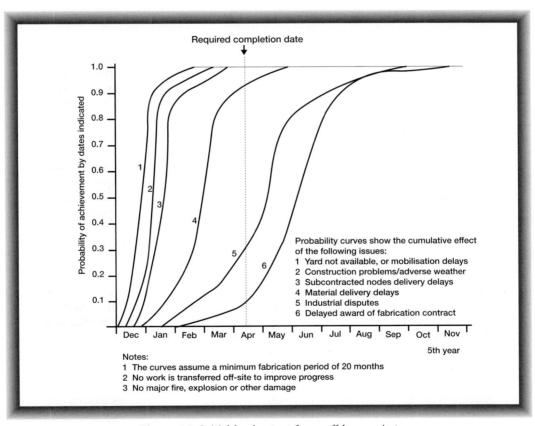

Figure 4.3 *Initial-level output for an offshore project*

maximises the insight provided. The downside is the large amount of data that is required to build the model and the time taken for the analysis.

Some people find approaches based on P-I matrices easier to use during the estimate phase, but they do not lend themselves to effective evaluation of project risk, either at an overall or intermediate level. The single-parameter risk index approach loses track of expected outcomes and project risk. Some users of P-I matrices focus on individual risk events on a first pass, omitting the first-pass Assess–Estimate sub-phase. Those who focus on risk events on the first pass are usually happy with a P-I matrix representation, but those who focus on project risk require a probabilistic approach.

A minimalist approach combines the relative simplicity of a box in a P-I matrix framework specific to each risk with a traditional probabilistic combination which estimates both expected values and associated contributions to project risk. This minimalist approach is designed for the use of an Evaluate–Estimate sub-loop (refer to Figure 4.2), and can be used to refine estimates for risk events which seem to matter (obtaining data to confirm their size, for example), before a loop back to the Define Project phase for a second pass.

Most experienced users of any probabilistic approach make selective use of an Evaluate–Estimate sub-loop in this way, avoiding collecting data when this would be expensive until it is clear that the data will be useful.

Whichever approach is adopted, the second pass through the risk management process as a whole will be shaped by the insight gained by the end of the first pass, and the Assess–Evaluate sub-phase is central to this shaping of further passes as well as to understanding project risk. A second pass will be necessary unless a first pass provides a convincing case for no further effort.

Plan Responses

Some people associate a first pass through the **Plan Responses** phase with the response planning aspects of all earlier sub-phases, there being no need for a separate Plan Responses phase *per se*. Alternatively, this phase can be seen as a separate set of tasks, such as the clarification of trigger conditions for implementing contingency responses. This *Guide* includes a Plan Responses phase which is divided into **Plan Risk Event Responses** and **Plan Project Risk Responses** sub-phases.

The focus of the **Plan Risk Event Responses** sub-phase is 'specific responses' associated with individual risk events. Looking for these responses can begin as early as the Identify phase, but it must begin no later than the end of the first cycle through the Assess–Evaluate sub-phase, the starting point shown on Figure 4.2.

The focus of the **Plan Project Risk Responses** sub-phase is project risk associated with the joint effect of specific responses plus 'general responses' associated with the collective management of overall risk. For example, it may be feasible to double- or triple-shift an activity in order to overcome the accumulated delays of earlier activities. A good general rule is to have at least one powerful general response available. Figure 4.2 shows the Plan

Project Risk Responses sub-phase starting at the end of the first sub-cycle through the Estimate–Evaluate sub-loop. This is the earliest point at which it is likely to receive attention. A systematic search for specific responses which can be treated as general responses and a follow-on search for other general responses as part of the second pass through the Assess–Structure phase is an effective point at which to start the Plan Project Risk Responses sub-phase.

The integration of both sub-phases of the first pass of the Plan Responses phase with earlier sub-phases is a matter of degree; what matters most is what gets done, rather than the sub-phase it is assigned to.

AN EXAMPLE: SECOND COMPLETE CYCLE OF STRATEGIC-LEVEL RISK MANAGEMENT

Initiate

A second pass through the **Initiate–Define Project** sub-phase will usually involve adjustments to basic project definition framing assumptions because of surprises revealed by the first pass. For example, the first-pass analysis may suggest an important design change because a construction risk event is best dealt with in this way, and thinking in these terms may suggest further opportunities associated with integrated design–construct issues not considered earlier.

A second pass through the **Initiate–Focus Risk Management Process** sub-phase will usually involve adjustments to the risk management plan because of surprises revealed by the first pass. For example, the first pass may suggest much more (or less) effort will be appropriate than that anticipated earlier. Project risk management processes are themselves high-risk projects which require responsive and flexible management.

Even if there are no significant surprises on the first pass, the objectives of the second pass may be quite different, requiring process changes. For example, the first pass may be largely about quantifying uncertainty – that is, to see if it matters and, if it matters, where it is most important. The second pass may be about careful response planning – that is, testing and choosing response strategies – in those areas which seem to matter most. Mature users will blur the distinction between the first and second passes to some extent. However, if an organisation and the individuals involved are not very experienced in risk management processes, clear changes in focus are useful.

The Identify phase

The **Identify** phase on the second pass might focus on a rich set of alternative responses for key risks not addressed by changes in Initiate–Define Project assumptions.

Assess

The **Assess–Structure** sub-phase on the second pass should continue the robust testing of earlier structuring decisions, but a richer set of tasks becomes relevant. For example, it is important to find out whether any of the specific responses already generated for particular risk events can deal with sets of risk events, making them general responses, and more powerful, as indicated earlier. At this point, a wider search for general responses may also be useful. Such responses might include starting a project three months earlier than planned to deal with any combination of risk events, including risk events which have not been identified, and so building in flexibility. It may also be a good idea to order the risks – for example, to reflect the sequence in which they may occur. And it will also be important to order responses in terms of preference.

The second-pass **Assess–Ownership** sub-phase for a project involving a number of subcontractors might look at the risk and response structure developed so far in order to define those parcels of work to be bid as packages. The aim here should be to avoid managing responses to contractor A's problem via contractor B, because of the obvious problems and costs associated with managing risks across contractual boundaries.

Whichever approach was taken on the first-pass estimation, the second-pass **Assess–Estimate** sub-phase involves traditional probabilistic models. Some argue that the additional effort required to transform a PIM-based first pass to a probabilistic second pass is a barrier to the multiple pass approaches which are needed, but this remains an unresolved point of contention, and organisations will need to make a careful evaluation of this issue.

On the second pass and subsequent passes there is general agreement that a probabilistic quantitative approach to quantifying risk events and evaluating alternative responses is essential. The Assess–Evaluate sub-phase of earlier passes will identify aspects of the project that are particularly uncertain. The Assess–Estimate phase of later passes may try to reduce this uncertainty by searching for appropriate data or using more sophisticated estimation techniques. However, the key to effective response planning is managing the risk. If risk can be contained, measuring it accurately may not matter, and 'show stoppers' clearly need managing, not measuring.

The second-pass **Assess–Evaluate** sub-phase can use diagrams like that shown in Figure 4.3 to manage further passes by highlighting where a deeper understanding of the causal structure of risk events would be useful. However, the focus can shift to the use of diagrams like that shown in Figure 4.4 to help make choices between alternative response assumptions.

If cost is the objective of interest (other objectives being assumed to be unaffected for the moment) a diagram like Figure 4.4 is a useful way of clarifying the basis for recommended response management choices. Choice A is said to be 'risk-efficient', in the sense that it dominates choices B and C, because its curve is entirely to the left of the curves for B and C. Choice A involves a lower expected cost – that is, lower than our best measure of

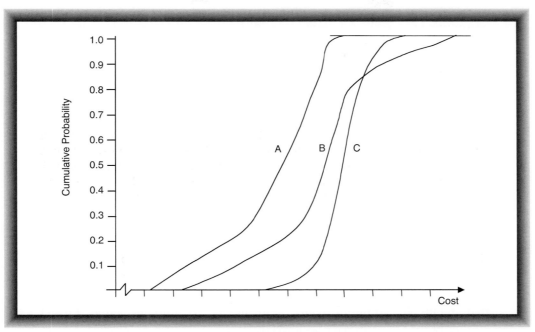

Figure 4.4 *S-curve of alternative responses*

what should happen on average. Choice A also involves less project risk, in that it has a lower probability of exceeding any given cost. Variability of cost, in itself, is not a direct measure of risk, because expected outcomes are relevant, but the dominance of B and C by A is clear. If choice A is not available, B involves less expected cost, but more risk, than C, and is the best choice depending on the organisation's ability to take risk on specific decisions or projects and average out the variations over the long haul. Taking more risk on individual decisions can result in more return/less long-haul risk, an issue involving a corporate view of risk efficiency as well as a project view.

If multiple attributes are involved (like time, cost and 'quality'), diagrams in the Figure 4.4 format remain the easiest framework for making response management choices. However, two or more diagrams for each choice will be required – one for each attribute.

Plan Responses

At the second pass the **Plan Responses** phase is best considered as being largely integrated with all the preceding sub-phases, as implied by Figure 4.2. For example, the question of trigger conditions associated with the cost-effective use of both specific and general responses will require careful attention to the impact of design changes and other Initiate–Define Project assumptions as well as Identification, Structure and Ownership sub-phase issues. However, it is important to ensure that all aspects of response planning relevant to this pass are complete before using the Assess–Evaluate sub-phase results to plan a further iteration if necessary. Ensuring that this is indeed the case is a useful role for this phase, as assumed here.

AN EXAMPLE: THIRD COMPLETE CYCLE OF STRATEGIC-LEVEL RISK MANAGEMENT

Initiate

A third pass through the **Initiate–Define Project** sub-phase may involve extensive and fundamental revisions if the second-pass Assess–Evaluate phase reveals problems that have not been resolved by response planning during the second pass. For example, a design many have to be revisited because the cost, as now understood, is far too high or original quality objectives may need to be fundamentally revised for similar reasons. If this is the case, more than three iterations through the whole process might be anticipated. On the other hand, it may have become clear after the second pass that relatively straightforward adjustments to Initiate–Define Project assumptions will suffice, as assumed here.

A third pass through the **Initiate–Focus Risk Management Process** sub-phase may also involve extensive and fundamental revisions if the second pass has revealed significant unresolved problems. On the other hand, it may be clear that relatively modest changes in process for the third pass, anticipated earlier, are all that is required, as assumed here.

Identify

The third-pass **Identify** phase might involve a search for previously overlooked key 'secondary' risks and responses – risk events associated with responses that are being relied on to deal with risk. For example, if a contracted resource becomes unavailable, and the response depends on contracting an alternative, will one be available? The target deliverable for this sub-phase is the identification of all key risk events – both threats and opportunities – and all relevant responses, classified, characterised, verified and reported.

Assess

The **Assess–Structure** sub-phase on the third pass might continue with general testing, for robustness, but also move on to the use of risk and response diagrams to help explain to users of the risk analysis process results how responses are ordered, how secondary risks trigger secondary responses, and how the specific and general response distinction operates. Such diagrams are summary decision trees, with decisions linked to risk events and response choices (See Appendix A.3.5). The target deliverable for this sub-phase is a clear understanding of the implications of any important simplifying assumptions about relationships between risk events, responses and base plans.

The **Assess–Ownership** sub-phase on the third pass – assuming it is a final pass – should allocate named individuals to the management of risk events and ensure that the associated financial implications have clearly defined owners. The target deliverable for this sub-phase is clear financial and managerial ownership allocations, effectively and efficiently defined, and legally enforceable in practice where appropriate.

The third-pass **Assess–Estimate** sub-phase might refine the shape of all probability distributions to ensure that any crude approximations used earlier do not attract unwarranted attention, in addition to making substantive final refinements. Where it is now clear that uncertainty about probabilities is important, data acquisition might prove useful to verify subjective judgements used earlier. This sub-phase builds on all earlier sub-phases to provide a basis for understanding what matters most, for making choices, and for predicting associated outcomes in terms of expected values and associated project risk.

The third-pass **Assess–Evaluate** sub-phase might ensure that diagrams of the form of Figure 4.3 build up to a final overall cost level in a way that can be presented top-down to explain what is driving project risk in cost terms, with similar diagram structures for time and key quality measures. It might also ensure that key project decision choices and recommendations can be explained in terms of diagrams in the Figure 4.4 format. If this is the final pass at the Assess–Evaluate phase for this risk management cycle, this sub-phase must provide a basis for seeking approval to proceed to the implementation phase of the project life cycle and begin detailed planning for project execution. This sub-phase should bring together the information accumulated by all previous sub-phases in order to provide a diagnosis of important risk and responses to it and to make a case for the proposed base plans and contingency plans.

Plan Responses

The third pass of the **Plan Responses** phase must be integrated with all earlier third-pass sub-phases, but ensuring the delivery of everything needed to gain approval for strategic-level base plans and associated contingency plans can be a useful focus for this sub-phase if seeking approval is to follow, as assumed here.

PLANNED ITERATIONS AND UNPLANNED ITERATIONS

The three strategic-level risk management cycles assumed for Figure 4.2 illustrate planned iterations. The discussion that followed should make it clear that they are planned because, when the project risk management process starts, there is limited information about what is important so that time cannot be effectively allocated to a simplistic one-pass (linear) approach. An approach involving planned iterations is essential if time is to be used effectively and efficiently.

In practice, however, unplanned iterations will need to be undertaken. Hence, a degree of reactive risk management is required, as well as proactive risk management. A reasonable professional judgement can be made to resolve the difficulties uncovered on the first pass with a set of responses developed on the second pass, but this judgement may prove incorrect. If the third pass has to start by redefining the project in significant ways, three passes may not be enough.

THE IMPLEMENT RESPONSES PHASE

There is no point in running all the earlier phases in the risk management process if the planned responses are not implemented. In the context of strategic-level project risk management the Implement Responses phase focuses on ensuring that strategic plans are changed to reflect all earlier risk management, and this is fully reflected in any related project-sanction process and associated arrangements. Later, if detailed plans are being implemented, the Implement Responses phase may involve ensuring that those responsible for specific responses do what is required.

Figure 4.2 shows the Implement Responses phase starting at the end of the first complete cycle, getting on with changes to strategic plans and associated arrangements as soon as possible once it is clear what has to be done and appropriate approvals are in place.

THE MANAGE PROCESS ACTIVITY

The risk management process itself needs to be managed and also integrated into the wider project management process. This involves monitoring progress, control in the sense of contingency plan implementation, control in the sense of looping back to the Initiate–Define Project sub-phase at strategic or detailed tactical plan levels, and rolling forward the detailed plans produced in the Plan Responses phase. Crisis management, which may involve revisions to strategic-level plans, is rarely eliminated, and it is prudent to make provision for it, but a risk management process should deliver a cost-effective balance between proactive and reactive risk management.

FOLLOW-ON DETAILED PLANNING AND ONGOING RISK MANAGEMENT

For strategic-level risk management purposes, most organisations find it useful to have 5–50 activities, depending on the complexity of the project and the contractual structure. For detailed tactical planning purposes, 50–5000 activities may be appropriate, to clarify who is doing what and when at a level of detail essential to implement a project. The number of activities will vary according to the kinds of project being dealt with. The key point, which applies equally to all organisations, is the scale change involved. Figure 4.2 is restricted to strategic-level planning, but a follow-on detailed planning process is usually essential.

In the simplest case, detailed planning within the sanctioned strategic plan is deterministic: the implementation stage of the project life cycle begins with a deterministic detailed planning process which makes full use of earlier risk management process outputs without any need for further formal risk analysis.

Usually, it is useful to refine some aspects of the detailed tactical plans necessary to implement a project through a further application of the risk management process. This can be envisaged as going back to the Initiate–Define Project sub-phase to redefine the project at a detailed planning level, then using the Initiate–Focus Risk Management Process sub-phase to adjust the process to the resulting detailed plans, and then carrying on with further iterations of this redefined risk management process. However, it is very important to see this revised process as being integrated with detailed planning in the implementation stage of the project life cycle, and not as part of the earlier pre-sanction strategic-level iteration structure. Looping back to redefine the strategic plan after approval for the plan is obtained, because 'the devil was in the detail', is an unplanned and highly undesirable outcome.

Detailed tactical-level plans need not be prepared for the whole duration of the project at this point. It is important to choose planning horizons for detailed plans which cope with all necessary lead time issues, but avoid detailed planning which will probably prove redundant. For example, in a five-year project, detailed plans for the use of critical resources may need a one-year planning horizon, but non-critical resources may need much less. Effective use of a risk management process can release time previously used for long-term detailed planning and make better use of it for risk management.

Ongoing use of the risk management process for project risk management once 'the planning is over and action begins' is a very important part of managing a project. The boundary is never clear, and planning never ends, but the Initiate-Focus Risk Management Process sub-phase and the Manage Process activity must reflect the impact of the changes in life cycle stage as project implementation progresses.

INITIAL USE OF RISK MANAGEMENT EARLIER OR LATER IN THE PROJECT LIFE CYCLE

If a risk management process is introduced in the conception stage, with a complete risk management cycle as portrayed by the whole of Figure 4.2 towards the end of this stage, managing the process will be more difficult because a clear design and activity structure at a strategic level will not yet exist. But, properly done, it will be more effective, because early misconceptions can be revealed and corrected before design and activity based plans are based on them. In these circumstances the nature of the process should be very different. The focus will be on the business case, and assumptions about revenue and contractual strategies may be central. Early use of sensitivity analysis, rather than probabilistic analysis, is often effective. It may also be useful to use aspects of other processes which address business case issues directly, such as Risk Analysis and Management for Projects (RAMP).

If a risk management process is introduced during the conception stage, with a second complete risk management cycle towards the end of the feasibility stage, the second cycle can build on the first, with a focus on strategic design choices and strategic planning in terms of activity-based plans. This is the recommended approach as, in this way, subsequent complete risk management cycles in later stages can continue to build on firm foundations.

If a risk management process is introduced for the first time in the implementation stage, after detailed planning has taken place, it will be very difficult to influence any strategic decisions. Furthermore, starting to use a risk management process in a project that is already being executed and in trouble is a very high-risk operation that is best avoided unless the analysts have sufficient experience to cope and high-level champions are available to ensure that appropriate corrective actions are taken.

MATURITY

The maturity of an organisation's project risk management processes is a function of its experience and the extent to which it has improved its capability via that experience and other learning processes. In this sense, maturity will influence important process choices within the overall risk management process. For example, organisations with a long history of effective and efficient use of project risk management usually employ probabilistic modelling as a central part of their process, but organisations lacking this facility often find it very difficult to get beyond P-I matrices. This makes it inherently difficult for them not only to make risk-efficient choices in an effective manner, but also to manage expectations in terms of the difference between expected outcomes, associated targets and commitments, and the provisions and contingencies which link these three values.

Organisations which adopt any project risk management approach should think explicitly and carefully about developing their maturity. Some guidelines are provided in Chapter 8 under 'Risk Maturity Models', but two issues need emphasis here.

First, it is important to see all applications of risk management as a learning process. That is, some of the effort expended is to plan the project in hand, but some of it is aimed at improving the organisation's planning capability for all future projects. If no investment is made in future capability, no progress will be made. This is particularly obvious when organisations first introduce formal project risk management processes. If they choose a trial project which is well planned to date, with some interesting high-profile decisions to make, and analyse it carefully and comprehensively, with external expert advice on process issues, they can understand where complexity is effective for providing insight and where simplification would be a better option. They can then test the effectiveness of shortcuts and more sophisticated approaches on subsequent trial projects and quickly evolve an effective and efficient approach to all projects of a given type which they have experienced. This is the recommended approach to introducing risk management for organisations with limited experience of effective and efficient formal project risk management processes. On the other hand, if an organisation chooses a trial project which is in trouble, perhaps introducing a formal risk management process for the first time as a quick fix because a bank or a regulator has required it, without advice from someone who has a mature view of what is needed, the risk management process is likely to fail along with the project. Treating risk management as a learning process is a less obvious need for organisations that have been doing it for years, but it remains important even if they are clearly leaders in the field and defining the leading edge. The leading edge is moving fairly quickly in some areas, particularly the trend to keep things simple without being simplistic.

Second, it is important to see risk management as a generic process to be adapted to each organisation's projects as part of the learning process. Making it more specific makes it more efficient. However, making it too specific can make it ineffective if a wider scope is required. The trick is to avoid making it so specific to today's projects that it becomes inappropriate for those of tomorrow.

ALTERNATIVE PERSPECTIVES

This chapter has discussed the risk management process from the perspective of a client. Contractors can apply all of the above to their view of a project and relate it to their client's view. In addition, clients may find it useful to study their contractors' perspective to understand the implications of alternative approaches to contracting, especially those involving partnering. Regulators and financiers – for example, banks and other interested parties may also use a risk management process, and sometimes their perspectives may be usefully studied by others.

CONCLUSION

This chapter has outlined how the five-phase risk management process could be applied in a generic project life cycle. Performing risk management at a strategic and then tactical level ensures that appropriate effort is used in relation to the stage the project has reached. The importance of iterating the risk management process has been illustrated using three sub-cycles at the strategic level.

The risk management process can be tailored to suit any project. Like any process, careful consideration must be given to adapting it for use. Every phase of the process must be undertaken; it is how it is undertaken that now needs to be considered.

5

Organisation and Control

This chapter describes issues of control and governance, and the resources, roles and organisation required to ensure effective risk management within the project and the business.

OVERVIEW

The introduction of risk management into an organisation requires careful planning to yield maximum benefits. It should be treated as a project and be subject to basic project management principles. These include defining aims (what you wish to achieve by introducing risk management) and monitoring achievement against those aims (see Chapter 7 for guidance on applying risk management). The organisational issues that need to be addressed to enable the required benefits to be delivered are discussed in this chapter. These issues apply to projects involving a single organisation or projects involving a number of different organisations and include responsibilities, roles and how risk changes throughout the project life cycle.

Resourcing is also discussed in this chapter because risk management consumes resources both in its introduction and operation, and these resources must be defined and allocated. They will include human resources and, in some cases, specialist tools to assist with the process. The cost of risk management should be only a small percentage of the overall project management expenditure and can result in benefits far exceeding its start-up and running costs.

Finally, the chapter discusses control issues, including documentation, risk data collection, reporting and reviews.

ORGANISATIONAL STRUCTURE

Planning for risk management

Setting up a risk organisation and control structure requires initial planning. It is wise to produce a risk management plan, an outline structure of which

49

is shown in Figure 5.1. The plan makes it quite clear how risk is going to be tackled for the project and refers to the risk management process and the risk management organisation. In many organisations it may be held as a template in the standard project methodology, although the risk management plan will always be specific to a particular project.

Alongside the introduction of risk management into an organisation, staff should be formally educated about the benefits of risk management, the reasons for its introduction and in the use of the tools and techniques that they will be expected to use on their projects. Understanding risk management and why it is being introduced will reduce people's scepticism and resistance to its introduction.

Contents:

1 INTRODUCTION

2 PROJECT DESCRIPTION
A brief description of what the project is for and its key parameters of success.

3 PURPOSE AND SCOPE OF RISK MANAGEMENT
The aims and objectives of the risk management process being applied to the project in question. What is, and is not, included within the scope.

4 RISK MANAGEMENT ORGANISATION
The specific responsibilities of people in the organisation who will be involved in risk management work. Clarification of the roles/responsibilities between the organisation, its client and its subcontractors.

5 RISK MANAGEMENT PROCESS
A description of the risk management process adopted for the project.

6 KEY DELIVERABLES

Annexes:

A INTRODUCTION TO RISK MANAGEMENT
Explanations of risk management, including definitions of risk and categories of risk.

B TOOLS AND TECHNIQUES
A description of those tools and techniques selected for use on this project.

C PROFORMA
Copies of standard forms used in the risk management process – for example, summary sheet and risk register.

Figure 5.1 *Suggested risk management plan contents*

Responsibilities

For the risk management process to be effective risk management responsibilities must be sufficiently defined and resourced. The extent of the risk management process needs to be considered. Will it comprise a company- or organisation-wide standard or will it be adaptable to each project situation? If the former, will some risk roles be permanently established, such as a corporate or divisional risk manager? There may, for example, be a permanent programme or project office that will perform risk-related roles for projects.

For a particular project, the day-to-day *accountability* for risk management usually rests with the project manager, who must ensure that risk is appropriately tackled within the project. However, *responsibility* for task-level risk would normally be delegated to others within the project or within the business, together with the necessary authority to control it. Although individuals at functional levels will be better placed to identify, understand and manage specific risks, the project manager will probably take responsibility for tackling project-level risks – that is, those risks that affect the project as a whole. The executive sponsor and project board (if appointed) will be responsible for deliberating on risks referred to them by the project manager.

Risk management is a professional role, and, for some projects, it will be necessary to appoint additional risk specialist roles to give support to the project manager. These may be a risk manager, a risk process manager or a risk facilitator, for example. In this case, it is important that the project manager does not relinquish accountability for risk within the project, but remains in control, delegating a level of authority to the supporting risk roles.

All this means that the risk management process must clearly state who is to be involved and at what levels, together with their level of authority. Figure 5.2 shows responsibilities for risk from the project level through to the top of a company or organisation.

Of course, no company or organisation will be exactly like that depicted in Figure 5.2. The levels between the board of an enterprise and a programme or individual project may be few or many. There may or may not be programme directors, project directors, steering groups or various types of project board. Nevertheless, whatever the structure, it is important to ensure that there is a flow of risk information throughout the organisation. This information may be in terms of costs and funding as well as threats and opportunities to the business as a whole.

Where projects involve a number of different external organisations, some risks may be shared between them, thus requiring the exact nature of risk-sharing to be defined. The ultimate responsibility for risk can be considered to rest with the client organisation because, in most projects, the client will lose most if the project fails (see Figure 5.3). Client organisations will try to penalise suppliers for failure to meet contract requirements, but the level of

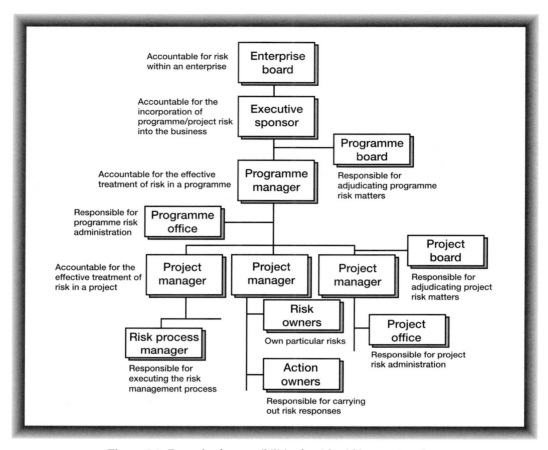

Figure 5.2 *Example of responsibilities for risk within an enterprise*

penalties is unlikely to reflect the loss of utility experienced by the client organisation. For this reason, it is usual for client organisations to ensure that suppliers employ risk management as an integral part of their project management procedures and, in some cases, to actively audit the supplier's risk management process.

A key purpose of risk management is to communicate the picture of the project's future and to provide the necessary level and detail of information to enable informed decisions to be made. Risk management requires an open environment within an information-aware, blame-free culture. Sponsors and stakeholders must be prepared to accept good as well as bad news concerning risks. If bad news is not accepted and not dealt with in a positive way then the risk management process could be undermined.

In assigning responsibilities (in either a single organisation project or a multi-organisation project) it is important to ensure that the responsible

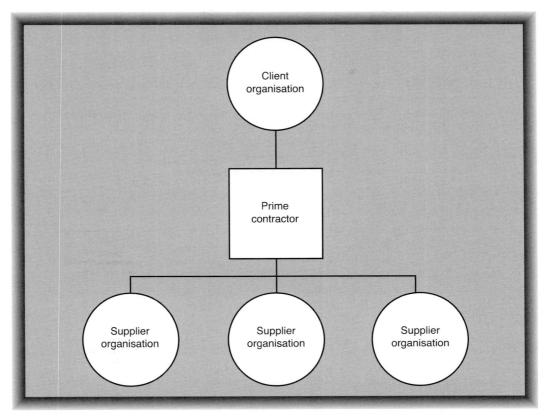

Figure 5.3 *Simple risk relationships in a multi-organisation project*

parties not only have sufficient control over the causes of their risk, but also have effective and practicable plans for dealing with risks that may materialise. An early assessment of risk can assist in the clarification of responsibilities and, in the case of a project where there is a potential for complex risk interfaces, enable these interfaces to be understood and complexity avoided where possible. Where this is not possible, considerable care is needed in drafting contracts to prevent the responsibility for managing the risks reverting to the client.

Recent developments in contracting strategies, such as the Private Finance Initiative and Public–Private Partnerships, have reduced the need for client organisations to manage complex risk interfaces by emphasising service delivery and combining the major stages of a project life cycle in one contract. These contracting strategies have increased the risk that is transferred to the prime contractor and suppliers, and there is a consequent need to balance the level of risk transfer and value for money.

Functional roles

Within an organisation, risk management should be treated as a team effort and, to be effective, requires regular interaction between various parts of the organisation. The risk-thinking team is a powerful force for affecting the outcome of the project. Risk management is not an activity that should be left to one or two people updating a risk register. Various functional roles are outlined below and can be used as the basis for terms of reference for individual team members.

The project manager's role

The project manager is effectively the champion of the risk management process for the project. Accountable for proper and effective risk identification and response, he or she needs to ensure that the entire project team is actively engaged in the process. This extends to suppliers and contractors, whose buy-in to the overall process is essential. The project manager needs to be assured of reliable data on which to make decisions regarding the project's progress and finances, for example. He or she also needs to have in place an adequate mechanism for reporting risk progress to senior management.

The project manager's role includes:

- agreeing and promoting the risk management process for the project
- clarifying the acceptable level of risk for the project
- reporting risk status to the client/senior management on a regular basis
- escalating risks that are above the risk threshold or risks with a significant impact outside of the project
- sanctioning the validity of the risk data
- chairing risk review meetings
- approving risk response actions
- monitoring the effectiveness of risk management in the project team.

The risk process manager's role

In many companies and organisations the risk process manager's role is routinely contained within that of the project manager. However, occasionally it is seen as beneficial to use a professional risk process manager, who is able to view a project against a background of experience.

The risk process manager, sometimes also known as the risk coordinator, risk specialist and other titles, will have a broad knowledge base, encompassing a range of business and technical issues. He or she may act as a facilitator, having an appreciation of the project's domain, rather than necessarily being an expert in its technical composition. Alternatively, a risk facilitator may be brought in from outside the project team to provide an independent view.

Reporting to the project manager, the role of the risk process manager is to facilitate the whole risk management process including:

- development of the risk management plan
- facilitating the identification and response of project risk
- collecting and normalising risk information from project staff
- mentoring project staff on aspects of the risk management process
- ensuring that the risk register contains data in a consistent format
- analysing risk data and directing the production of risk reports
- facilitating risk assessment reviews and workshops
- advising the project manager on risk response options
- reviewing the progress of risk response actions
- contributing to the presentation of risk for senior management.

The risk manager's role

A professional risk manager is occasionally required to take responsibility for the identification and assessment of risk and response to it. It is a role sometimes required for a programme of projects and risk-sensitive projects, and may be carried out either on a full-time or consultative basis. Depending on project scale and scope, it may be possible for a risk manager to also absorb the role of risk process manager.

A risk manager would not only look for the best business responses to risk but also for opportunities arising from risks. His or her ability to think laterally and see the big picture of risk is an important consideration. Construction of worst-case risk scenarios and decision trees (see Appendix A.3.5) are examples of the regular assessment work that a risk manager would undertake.

A risk manager would, for example, assist a project board in making decisions such as whether to curtail testing and launch the new product early in order to be ahead of the competition or show the best option for implementing a project change.

The risk owner's role

The risk owner is a temporary role that may be performed by any member of the project team or by a specialist from outside the project (that is, within the organisation or business as a whole). The project manager assigns risk owners to be accountable for one or more identified risks. Risk owners are selected according to their affinity with particular risk types or environments. For example, someone with an affinity with networking would be best placed to own a risk concerning the development of a wide-area network.

Risk owners:

- liaise with people who are raising a risk to ensure that it is properly expressed and sufficiently understood
- ensure that expertise is provided to effectively assess a risk and develop suitable responses.

They may either act as experts themselves or may procure expertise as required. They will also recommend action owners, who will develop responses for the risks for which they are accountable.

The action owner's role

Like that of a risk owner, an action owner's role is a temporary one that may be performed by any member of the project team or by a specialist from outside the project. Action owners are assigned either by the project manager or risk manager directly or as recommended by risk owners. They are responsible for carrying out actions in response to one or more risks. There may be several action owners with respect to a single risk. Risk owners may also elect to carry out some actions themselves, depending on suitability (see 'Resourcing risk response actions' (p. 58) for further information).

The technical specialist's role

Both within and outside a project there may be various technical specialists whose input to the risk management process could be vital. Often taking on the temporary role of risk owner, technical specialists will often be the only people able to estimate the degree of probability or impact for identified risks. Similarly, they may be best placed to recommend risk treatment actions when considering risk responses.

The role of the technical specialist therefore includes:

- identifying and raising risks for work within their domain
- assuming the role of risk owner for one or more risks
- giving expert opinion for the identification, evaluation and treatment of risk
- personally carrying out risk treatment actions, where assigned, in the role of action owner.

Other functional roles

Besides the project team, who need to be continually involved in the risk management process, there are other roles within the company or organisation that will also need to be involved, depending on their function. If a project has identified a list of stakeholders, then each stakeholder role will need to be examined in terms of its contribution to the risk management process.

For example, the finance manager would be interested in any contingency provisions being requested as a result of risk responses, and also whether the project risk exposure is increasing or decreasing. The contracts manager needs to understand the implications of risk treatment actions on project contracts. The legal department needs to understand any business threats from identified risks and be involved in their mitigation. The sales function will be interested in any opportunities that may arise from planning responses to identified risks. Marketing will be particularly interested in any threatened damage to, or enhancement of, company reputation and will want to become involved in relevant risk treatment actions. Finally, customers or suppliers may specify the need to share risk information, and this may be a contractual provision.

The executive sponsor's role

The role of the executive sponsor, who is accountable for the incorporation of project risk into the business, includes:

- setting and monitoring risk thresholds for the project
- approving strategic risk response plans, which may include change of scope or approach (or cancellation) of the project
- reviewing escalated risks and approving proposed risk responses for these risks
- reviewing the effectiveness of risk management in producing information to support management decisions
- reporting risk status to senior management on a regular basis
- leading the management of risk at the business level (for example, where the impact or cause of the risk lies outside the project).

Risk management and the project life cycle

As a project moves through its lifespan, risk should be formally assessed at each stage, although the scope for influencing the overall outcome reduces as the project progresses. The general principle is to maintain a level of risk management effort throughout the project commensurate with the needs of the current phase and to focus this effort prior to project milestones where the level of commitment changes significantly (usually at the end of each project stage or phase). The decision on whether or not to proceed to a new level of commitment should then be based on an in-depth understanding of the associated risks. Some methodologies specify formal *gateway reviews,* where risk is formally reviewed at particular *stage gates* (such as feasibility or award of contract). However, it is important not to be complacent about risk between project phases or gates; risk management is an ongoing activity and the project team needs to think about risk in its daily activities. Whilst phase-ends are clearly targets for formal risk assessments, reviews and lessons-learned activities, they should not be the sole risk activity.

In terms of project life cycle, risk management begins at the conception stage during which the idea for the project will be thought through in commercial, as well as technical, terms. This stage usually results in a number of possible alternatives, and these should be assessed for their risks, costs and benefits.

The commercial viability of the project and its implications in terms of cost, timescale or performance are established during the feasibility stage. This is where risk management is at its most significant. Where high levels of uncertainty and impact exist, demonstration and prototyping may be undertaken as part of the risk management strategy. Thus, at the end of the feasibility stage a clearer understanding of, and in some cases a reduction of, the project risks clarifies the parameters of the decision-making process, allowing the project to proceed to the next stage, if the level of risk is acceptable to the organisation.

Risk management is particularly appropriate to contract tendering and bidding. A risk assessment can be made showing both an unmitigated risk exposure (that is, without the effect of mitigating actions) and a mitigated risk exposure, for comparison.

During the execution of the project work, regular risk assessments may be made, together with risk reviews targeted at phase or key milestone ends. Before any formal testing or piloting phase, risk assessment activity is particularly relevant. Testing itself will confirm or dispel risks associated with the product. Prior to project handover or implementation, any outstanding risks need to be reassessed, especially in terms of any ongoing support or maintenance work after the project has gone live.

Resourcing the risk management process

The level of resource commitment for risk management activities needs to be decided and specified in the risk management plan. The perceived level of risk activity will depend on the type of project. Projects that are concerned with highly innovative products or development work would need to give more emphasis to risk management. Likewise, projects with high health and safety considerations would need to give more emphasis to the reduction of the occurrence of such risks and minimising their impact should they occur.

Repeat projects have the luxury of precedence and can, therefore, gauge more accurately the level of risk management activity required. In all projects, it is more usual for the greatest concentration of risk resources to be at the start of a project, when familiarity with the work to be done is at its lowest.

Resourcing risk response actions

Resourcing risk response actions is work that is often left incomplete. Having identified and assessed risks, it is vitally important that actions are raised and that owners are assigned to carry them out. Further, the actions themselves must be able to demonstrate an effect on reducing the threat or increasing the opportunity – in other words, risk owners must estimate by the degree of change in probability and/or impact effected by carrying out each action.

Risk owners are responsible for ensuring that actions are properly expressed, that owners are assigned to carry out the actions (if not themselves), that each action has a due date and is costed, and that probability and impact changes are estimated.

Action owners should ensure that they have the time and skill required to carry out actions assigned to them and report progress against each action.

As actions usually cost time and money, they should also be linked to project task and activity schedules. Risk actions need to be validated against the project plan and included as tasks. In addition, the cost of risk response actions needs to be added to the project cost.

CONTROL

Risk documentation

Well-defined and concise documentation is essential to support the control of risk for the duration of a project. The main elements of such documentation will be as follows:

- **Risk management plan** – describing how risk will be addressed for the project (refer back to the guide given in Figure 5.1)
- **Risk register** – recording identified risks, probabilities, impacts, costs and priorities, together with risk reduction actions (examples are shown in Appendix A at Table A.2.4)
- **Risk analyses** – analyses of risk data
- **Risk reports** – documenting the status of risks, actions progress, etc.
- **Risk reviews** – formal risk review outcomes
- **Risk workshop output** – documenting the proceedings of risk identification or assessment group sessions
- **Risk lessons learned** – produced at major stage-ends or at project close-out.

The risk documentation forms part of the project documentation and should be subject to both the project's configuration management system and audit under the project's quality management activities.

Ideally, risk documentation should be centrally held and accessible to the project team via a shared database or intranet. If the risk register is held online, it is easier for team members operating remotely to raise or update risks and actions. Reports and analyses should be appended to a central file. Lessons learned should be appended to a company or organisation knowledge database. The risk management plan should state the provisions for appending and accessing risk documentation.

When considering risk documentation, it is important to also consider the uses to which it will be put. Risk data is vital for assisting the decision-making process, both within the project and within the business. As good decision-making relies on good data, the right quality of data must be collected through the risk management process. It is very easy to collect and record risk data that will never serve any useful management purpose.

Risk reporting

Risk information needs to flow from the project team to the project executive via the project manager and programme manager (if appointed), so that it can be integrated into the organisation's overall reporting cycle. It will also provide the main input for risk reviews that take place at critical decision points in the project.

It is good practice to include risk progress in the project's regular progress reports. This helps to maintain focus within the team and prevent risk management from becoming a once-a-quarter exercise.

Where there is an external client, it may be desirable (or in some cases mandatory) to pass the risk information to this organisation. This would normally be required in a predefined format, particularly if risk information from a number of suppliers must be combined. If this is the case, it is essential to ensure that the data has been derived consistently and according to the ratings specified in the risk management plan.

Risk reviews

Risk reviews provide a formal opportunity to examine and discuss the risk status of the project and to agree actions that will move the project towards meeting its overall aims and objectives. The project manager and the risk process manager should attend, possibly with representatives of key functions, such as contracts and finance, and senior technical staff.

In some public sector organisations risk reviews may take the form of a risk management review panel, risk working party or risk committee. In other sectors, the risk review may form part of a stage-end or phase-end review.

The risk review meeting agenda should include:

- a report by the risk process manager giving an overview of the major risk issues
- a review of the status of existing actions in place to reduce risk and the need for any new actions, a review of changes in risk status (that is, new risks, changes in risk levels, risks that have materialised and risks that have expired)
- a review of achievement at past milestones and predictions of future achievement.

The risk review concept can be applied to both single- and multi-organisation projects. It can also (within the limitations imposed by contractual relationships) form part of the agenda for meetings between stakeholding organisations.

In addition, the risk manager or project manager may call other meetings to discuss risk from time to time, and risk identification or risk assessment workshops may be usefully run for specific risk purposes.

Control of generic and project-specific risks

The control of risk requires the implementation of appropriate actions or measures. Project-specific actions can be carried out locally within the project, and periodic risk reviews provide the opportunity to check that these actions have been effectively implemented. Risks with actions that have a wider applicability than any one project should be communicated more widely. Initially, these risks and actions should form part of a library of generic risks and actions. In addition, the actions should be incorporated in procedures that apply to the whole organisation and will, over time, become part of normal business activities. This approach provides a suitable framework to address risk for the purpose of corporate governance and Internal Control (see Figure 5.4).

Risk governance

Risk governance is the ability to review and control the results of risk management activities in relation to a project, a programme of projects or the business as a whole. Any risk governance activity should therefore form part of an organisation's project governance. With increasing legislation being targeted at corporations to implement due diligence (for example, through recommendations from government reports such as Turnbull in the UK and Sarbanes-Oxley in the US), the need to establish governance processes at all management levels is now apparent.

Analysis of risk data can produce metrics for the control of risk on a monthly or similar regular basis. The level of risk exposure, for example, can be used to check the real costs of a project against progress. Typical data for risk governance should include:

- Monetary risk exposure (£RE)
    - £RE at project start
    - current £RE
    - target £RE
    - forecast £RE, month by month to project completion
- Contingency reserves
    - reserves at project start
    - position of unused reserves year-to-date
    - forecast of required reserves to project completion
- Risk tolerances
    - costs of risk reduction activity to date
    - forecast of costs to project completion

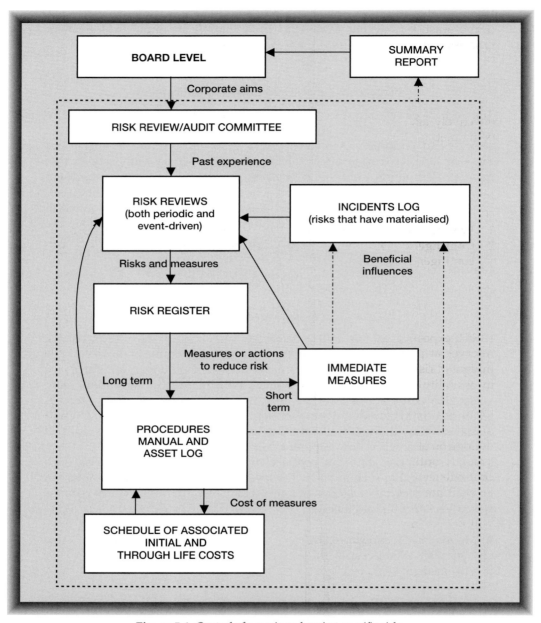

Figure 5.4 *Control of generic and project-specific risks*

One aspect of governance is audit. Targeted or scheduled audits may be carried out to ensure that the risk management process is being utilised effectively. In particular, an audit should ascertain the effectiveness of the process in meeting its aims as set out in the risk management plan. Measures meaningful to the aims of the process (for example, the occurrence of risks not forecast, probability, impact costs, overall risk exposure, cost effectiveness assessment for risk response, recording, retention of data, frequency of review of risks and actions) should be applied and reviewed. Audit should also consider whether achievement is being measured against forecast and whether planned actions are being implemented in a timely way.

The executive sponsor must be satisfied that the process is being managed effectively and that any corporate governance and audit requirements are being met.

Risk reserves

Risk reserves generally fall into two categories:

1 **Project reserves** – reserves made by the project for project exceptions.
2 **Contingency reserves** – reserves made specifically for funding risk contingency situations.

Additionally, a company may make reserves for emergency situations. These reserves are generally not allocated as a budget for business operational functions, but held for exceptional purposes, and not just for risk situations.

Risk exposure is a factor that can affect the determination of contingency reserves at project outset. If the unmitigated risk exposure is high but the mitigated risk exposure is low, much will depend on the organisation's faith in its ability to successfully reduce the risk, plus its general attitude to risk-taking. Setting aside the full amount of an unmitigated risk exposure, for example, demonstrates a low tendency towards risk-taking or low confidence in the ability to mitigate the risk.

Control of the risk reserves should be through the project governance process, outlined in the previous subsection. In some organisations the contingency is 'handed out' across the project team to be managed at lower levels. Care needs to be taken with this approach, as invariably the contingency reserve is based on the premise that some risks will happen and others will not – that is, the factored cost of the risk, (probability × cost), will be budgeted for, rather than the full cost. Consequently, the amount assigned to any one risk will generally not be adequate to pay for the risk materialising; it will need to be subsidised by money from the non-occurrence of other risks.

CONCLUSION

The introduction of risk management into an organisation, if well planned, provides a sound framework for controlling project risk. A clear statement of the aims of risk management, documented in a risk management plan, along with the definition of organisation, specific roles, thresholds and measures of success, will help to gain good value in return for investment in the process. It is especially important to be clear, from a risk management viewpoint, what is within the scope of the project, what is to be escalated to the programme or business level and the mechanisms for this escalation. In particular, the management of contingency reserves should be controlled through the governance process.

The relative priorities in the aims of risk management may change as the project progresses through its life cycle, so a refocus of risk management at each major stage may be considered. Finally, regular audit of the effectiveness of risk management will ensure that this focus is maintained throughout the life of the project.

6

Behavioural Influences

This chapter describes behavioural influences in a risk context, along with a variety of possible interpersonal approaches and some areas of particular concern to the risk manager and risk specialists.

INTRODUCTION

The behaviour of the involved individuals will have an impact throughout project risk management and will contribute directly to its success or failure. The project manager, the risk specialist, the project team, the client, the end user, the supplier – and, indeed, the whole supply chain – will influence identification, analysis, planning, decisions and action.

Each of these individuals, working alone or in groups, will have a unique interpretation of, and behaviour towards, risks. Every person has a unique personality, set of experiences and set of circumstances. Their behaviour – their reaction to this concoction – will be unique. Hence, what one person may identify, quantify and manage as a risk, the next may react to in a very different way. He or she may not even recognise the future event, may not consider it important or probable, or may decide to act/manage the situation differently.

The project manager should bear in mind that:

(a) the input to the project risk management process arises from the opinions of individual human beings

and

(b) much of the variances in performance in project risk management arises from the different views that people have when they identify and respond to risk.

Project managers and risk specialists will require not just the methods and techniques of project risk management but also effective people skills if they are to achieve their objectives of a project completed in time, to budget and to the required specification. No amount of 'applied guide', risk or otherwise, will work without these skills.

People skills may be inherent in our make up or they may be developed through processes of learning. The material presented here is aimed at giving practitioners a glimpse of some of the complex issues they may encounter. They are based on practical experiences of the contributors, and it is hoped that the information will help identify areas of potential ambiguity and complexity, leading to more sensitive and successful project risk management.

The main section of this chapter introduces the influences on an individual's behaviour and specifically his or her behaviour towards risks. The second section outlines a collection of individual interpersonal approaches which have been successfully employed to assist the risk manager with the planning and execution of project risk management. The final main section identifies four areas of particular concern: relationships with the risk specialists; risk transfer and allocation from customer to supplier; teamwork at enterprise level; and estimates and forecasting.

INFLUENCES ON BEHAVIOUR

The study of human behaviour cannot be distilled into one single chapter; more in-depth information can be obtained from the literature on organisational behaviour. However, there are important elements that influence behaviour towards risks, and these can usefully be discussed here.

Simply, as illustrated by Figure 6.1, human behaviour may be described as the result of a complex interaction between two distinct elements:

- the person themselves (perception, attitude, personality, motivation)
- the situation – both macro and micro environments (for example, the politics, the economics and the group/team, organisation).

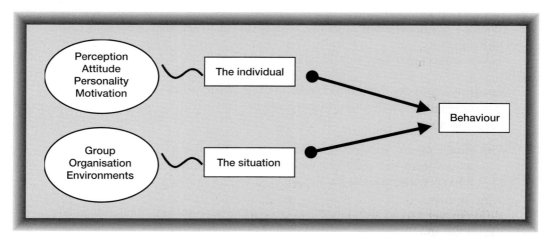

Figure 6.1 *A description of human behaviour*

Added to this is the further complication of time. Any or all of the elements described above may change today, tomorrow or in six months' time.

In an attempt to understand the uniqueness of an individual's behaviour, a brief explanation of these elements is offered below.

The constituents of the individual

Perception

Perception of risk is derived from a comparative view. An individual will select, reject and compare information against experience, and will tend to consider a risk event as either greater or less than another risk event. The individual's perception of risk is a composite of true uncertainty and lack of comparative knowledge.

In the context of project risk management this may manifest itself in several ways:

- 'Specialists' in a particular domain may perceive risks as being far greater in other domains with which they are less familiar. This may cause specialists to understate risks within their own domain and to over-emphasise other risks.
- Conversely, the 'specialist' closest to a potential risk may acknowledge the full measure of that risk, or even augment it, because of previous experiences. He or she may go on to deemphasise, or perhaps even reject, other potential risks as no previous connections have been made.
- However, the 'specialist' closest to the risk is the one most able to assess risk on the basis of true uncertainty, and the 'specialist' from another domain is most likely to overstate the risk due to lack of knowledge influenced by conjecture, hearsay and unsubstantiated opinion.
- Alternatively, a 'specialist' may trivialise or ignore risks suggested by someone outside his or her domain because this external opinion may be perceived as invalid.

Individual perceptions can lead to the denial of risks and a delay in managing them. Thus, there is a danger that a risk will be suppressed or, conversely, that an inflated risk will achieve undeserved credibility. As a result, the gap between perceived risk and actual risk will increase, with the potential for unforeseen risks to materialise with concomitant serious consequences for the project outcome.

Attitude

Attitude describes the persistent tendency to feel and behave in a particular way. Influenced by emotions, information and previous behaviour, it is different yet linked to belief (reality as it is understood), values (what is desirable) and motivation (rewards and protection of the ego). There are core attitudes which are resistant to change and peripheral attitudes which may change easily if further information or experience is added. Attitudes can be personal or shared within an organisation.

Attitude to risk is strongly linked to conditioning. For example, during a previous project an individual may have expressed an honest and objective view towards risk within his or her domain. However, he or she may have experienced a lack of support, even hostility, from the peer group, management and/or the organisation. Consequently, the individual will have received a 'bad' experience arising from that honesty. This conditioning (repeated bad experiences) may cause the individual to be reluctant to accept responsibility for risk in the future. Conversely, the individual who has worked within groups and organisations that have taken a positive attitude towards risk management will tend to be more positive and optimistic about the benefits when addressing this issue in the future. In extreme cases, the individual may exhibit an overconfident attitude.

Furthermore, an individual's conditioning towards risk may have taken place in a different organisation, perhaps years previously, and although it is not directly applicable to the current situation, it still impacts upon it.

The risk manager needs to identify such attitudes and either coax individuals back to an open and honest appraisal of the risks or instil a sense of responsibility.

Personality

Personality can be portrayed in two ways :

- by properties (traits, features or qualities – for example, extrovert or introvert, leadership style)
- by processes (the way we perceive, are motivated, learn, think, solve problems, relate to others, understand ourselves).

We inherit our personalities through our genes and we 'grow' them through experience.

In behaviour terms personality impacts on how we see ourselves and on how others see us, and the relationship – perhaps even conflict – that may arise if these perceptions are different.

Specifically in risk terms:

- Do I think I am a risk-taker or am I risk-averse? Do I usually act first and think later or do I consider all opportunities and threats before acting? How have my life experiences influenced these characteristics?
- Do you see me as a risk-taker or as risk-averse compared to yourself? Do I understand and condone your characteristics or are they alien to me?
- Am I happy with my state and does it fit with others working around me? If it does not, do I have strong leadership characteristics and do I wish to impose my risk-taking view on others? Or am I able to tolerate and adjust or conform to the majority or loudest view?

It can be seen, then, that personality has a strong impact on the way in which individuals identify and react to risk.

Motivation

As can be seen from Figure 6.2 motivation can be outlined as an internal driving force that impels individuals to achieve some goal in order to fulfil some need or expectation. Fulfilling this goal leads to a state of rest or satisfaction, which may be only temporary.

Motivation has fondly been interpreted as the 'personal agenda' and may be seen as underlying the political games played in the workplace. Whilst it is important for the project manager, risk facilitator and risk process

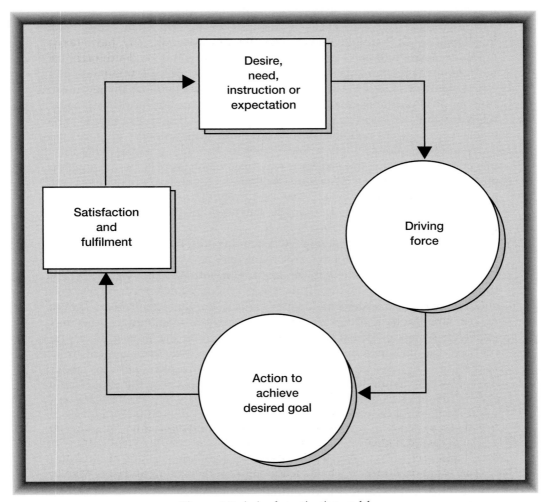

Figure 6.2 *A simple motivation model*

manager to be aware of, and consider, the 'personal agendas' of all the stake-holders, it should be borne in mind that:

- they will not always be obvious or public – indeed, part of the political game may be to keep them well hidden until an appropriate moment.
- they may be open to misinterpretation because both the risk facilitator and risk process manager bring their own perception and attitudes to their attempts at understanding others' 'personal agendas'
- they may be out of the sphere of influence of the risk facilitator or risk process manager.

The ability to motivate a project team to carry out risk management in a proactive manner, is the key to success for every project manager who wishes to deliver his or her project within the planned time, cost and performance objectives. This is particularly important when project risk management is first introduced into the project team: the individuals within the team will need to be motivated to change the way in which they work, and to begin managing risk. If individuals within a team are already overworked, they will need a strong motivator to ensure that they make time to do risk management properly. All too often, the project manager relies on the risk process and the risk process manager to motivate the team. All too often, people will just carry out the minimum they can get away with in order to show a token compliance. Such a scenario has serious consequences for the project risk management process, because generally it is the easy front-end process steps (risks identified, impact assessed, and risk treatment plans listed), that are carried out and the most important step that is usually omitted – namely, carrying out the actions to manage the risks.

A project manager who is respected and admired by his or her team can often be the best motivator for risk management – not just by expressing his or her personal wish that the team carry out risk management, but through his or her behaviours. If the project manager never informally asks about progress on risks but always focuses on today's problem, never makes time for risk at his or her project review meetings, cancels risk review meetings or doesn't turn up for them, then the project team will not perceive that their project manager considers risk management to be important. The project manager should informally ask questions about risks, always attend the risk review meetings, and drive the programme review meetings from a risk perspective. In this way, the project team will see from the project manager's behaviour that he or she thinks that risk is important and this in turn will motivate the team to put more effort in the management of risk.

In a similar way, the project executive sponsor can help motivate the team for risk management by underlining the importance of risk management in the wider business context and setting an example on how risk should be considered throughout the project.

The constituents of the situation

Returning briefly to the behaviour model (Figure 6.1), having described the elements of the individual, the influence of the situation must be considered. This can be observed at two levels:

- the macro level : the external environment characterised as the political, economic, social, technological influences
- the micro level: the immediate circumstances – that is, the group, team or organisation.

Figure 6.3 models these levels and suggests that the interfaces must also be considered.

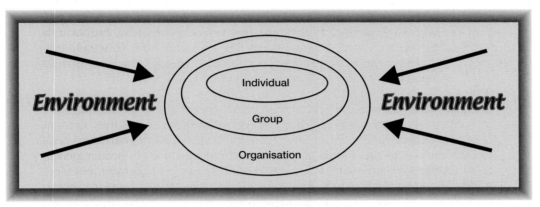

Figure 6.3 *Sources of situational influence*

Group influences

Some fairly simple issues can be highlighted. As we have seen, individuals react to the risk process in accordance with their 'perceptions' and 'attitudes' towards risk, and members of every project team will have had a wide range of previous experiences and knowledge. Project managers, risk facilitators and risk process managers must be mindful of this range and the complexity of its consequences, as this is likely to have an impact on risk information and bias conclusions.

An individual's behaviour is highly likely to be influenced by the collective attitude of the group (for example, the project team). Several states have frequently been observed and should be considered:

- Group-think or peer pressure within a risk-negative group will tend to suppress any individual who is prepared to operate in an open risk environment.

- Conversely, a 'risk-aware' group will tend to encourage the individual to take an open attitude towards risk.
- A group may tend to exhibit a more bullish attitude towards risk than any one of its constituent individuals. When involved in collective reasoning, they will tend to take more risky decisions without necessarily acknowledging that these decisions contain more risk. This may arise from one, two or all three of the following causes:
    - Collective responsibility for a decision reduces the probability that any one individual will be called to account for the decision(s) taken. An individual is therefore less inhibited by that responsibility and will tend to take the position that it was not his decision.
    - Individuals have a natural tendency to wish not to be negative within the group; they are sensitive to being charged with being 'gloom-and-doom merchants' or 'wet blankets'. These and similar phrases are common within the group psyche and lead to a suppression of candid observation.
    - Within a group there will often be a mixture of strong vocal extrovert characters and less vocal introvert ones. The introverts will tend to avoid confrontation whilst the extroverts may have a tendency to be unrealistically optimistic.

Such sweeping generalisations are simplistic in explaining the full measure of human behaviour within a group but there is sufficient credibility in them to give risk managers an insight into the complexities and to give them cause to treat the outcomes of such groups with circumspection. In particular, the third group behaviour might be exhibited while using project risk management techniques such as risk brainstorming sessions. The facilitator running such brainstorming sessions must judge the collective mood of the group and identify the 'quiet dissenters' for subsequent one-on-one discussions. If brainstorming sessions alone are used to assess probability and impact, it can be the most vocal individual's views which dominate.

Organisation influences

The next layer of influence towards risk is that of the organisation within which the individual/group exists. Again, much is known and has been written about organisations, and organisational behaviour in particular. It is a good idea to spend some time studying this body of knowledge. However, it suffices here to acknowledge that organisations range from being risk-averse to risk-takers in character.

For instance, organisations which have a responsibility for safety (say, the nuclear industry) or which have a long history of cautionary behaviour (say, insurance) will tend to have a risk-averse culture. Not only will individuals be discouraged from taking risks but they will also tend to avoid 'owning up' to the existence of a risk that they may have taken. In these organisations, risk-taking (and honesty about risks taken) is seen to be a career-limiting behaviour and, as such, is avoided by the individual.

Risk-taking organisations (software industries, advertising, oil, speculative investment and so on) tend to support individuals who have the courage and vision to back their hunches and launch themselves and their organisation into high-risk/high-reward strategies. The individual is encouraged to take risks and is rewarded on the basis of the aggregate outcome of those risks. Within these organisations risk-taking can become a 'macho' activity, with the risk-takers becoming distanced from the reality of the risks they take. The classic case is the speculative investor who gambles ever-larger sums on movements within the stock/ financial/futures markets until the risk impact becomes catastrophic.

These are extremes of organisational influence. All organisations in the supply chain will have a position on the risk-taking/risk-averse continuum and each will have a degree of influence in the project environment. This influence will affect the involved individuals and hence the risk manager's work.

The other factor that needs to be considered is that of upward reporting of risk data within an organisation. The manner in which senior management react to risk data shared with them by project teams will affect the quality of risk data reported by project teams on subsequent occasions. For example, if the management board overreacts to bad news, then the project team is likely to 'tone down' bad news for subsequent reports.

Environmental influences

At the macro level, the environment and culture can influence an individual's behaviour towards risk. Seminal works identify different national characteristics, although a specific focus on risk-taking/risk-averse behaviour is so far absent. The political, economical, social and technological status of a nation will influence the project risk management process from identification to management and control. Both the immediate and a long-term view must also be considered.

For example, when a project starts, the government may be risk-taking, relishing the risks associated with investment overseas, encouraging international prospecting and project-seeking, and rewarding individuals and businesses who do so. In such a culture the project team may be likely to ignore, scantily review or positively take risks if the rewards are significant. However, if a new government is elected mid-project term, a different view may be upheld. If the new government's direction is towards consolidating home assets, external activities may be penalised. In this case, previously identified risks may be valued very differently and 'new' risks may be identified, suddenly putting the project in jeopardy.

Interpersonal approaches

This section addresses some specific people skills that have been successful in project risk management. This is by no means an exhaustive list.

Preparation

There is no substitute for being fully prepared to facilitate a project risk management exercise. A project team will rapidly lose confidence in a facilitator who has not read up on the project's aims and objectives, who has little or no appreciation of the type, scale and importance of a project's requirements, and who is using the valuable time of the project staff to aid his own learning process.

Education

It is quite usual for project staff to be unclear about the objectives of the project risk management process and to thus treat them with caution or hostility. The risk process manager should accordingly take time at the beginning of the process to present the general mechanics and reasons for conducting project risk management. Not only the benefits, but the way in which they can be reduced if project risk management is not undertaken impartially, should be described. Care should be taken to ensure that staff understand that the exercise is not an attempt to apportion blame and that they can be honest and candid without fear of recrimination. The risk process manager should then explain exactly how the project risk management for this particular project is to be undertaken, what is expected from the staff, how they will be kept informed of the findings, what their responsibilities are and so on.

Facilitation

The risk facilitator's and risk process manager's role facilitates the mechanics of project risk management so that the project staff are free to contribute without hindrance and with the minimum of their time and energy. Project staff tend to be under time and resource pressures and can see project risk management as just a further demand made of them. The process should be organised quietly and simply, and contributors must be kept informed of housekeeping and administrative matters affecting them. Agendas must be distributed in advance and materials (flipcharts, overhead projectors, white boards etc.) must always be on hand without fuss. Documents must be short, clear, succinct and well distributed.

Early participation

As with the project as a whole, staff should be encouraged to participate in, become involved with and, more importantly, take ownership of the project risk management process as early as possible. At this stage it is very important that the project leader (normally the project manager) should be seen as a driving force.

Encouragement

The risk facilitator and risk process manager must not contribute to the assessment of risk but should encourage the project staff to think fully about the issues. A questioning style should be adopted, in order to help the contributors consider issues and place those issues in perspective. The contributor should be encouraged to take a lateral view, to think the 'unthinkable', and to avoid prejudicial views. A 'no blame' culture is important.

Relationships

The risk facilitator and risk process manager should not form judgements about individuals but should work to establish a personal relationship with each. To become trusted, they must be trustworthy and that means not expressing judgements or opinions about others within the team or about the project. They should respond to each individual in an unthreatening and cooperative manner.

Interviews

Where necessary, the risk process manager should meet with contributors on a one-on-one basis and spend some time getting to know their broader objectives, concerns and problems. This may give rise to knowledge about risks that the contributor is unhappy to express in open forum. The risk process manager should find other ways to ensure that such risks become accepted by the project.

Reporting

Whilst the risk process manager should be clear about the current views on project risks, it is likely that contributors and managers are less clear. The risk process manager should therefore take every opportunity to report to the project on the current position even where this might seem unnecessary or too frequent. Reports should be easy to understand, and major changes or concerns should be highlighted.

Group activities

A group activity, such as risk identification through brainstorming, is potentially a most valuable experience for the project and for each individual. Often such an activity represents one of the few times the project team gets a chance to think and interact freely.

Group activities enable different disciplines to understand the project from other viewpoints as well as the risks in other disciplines. They encourage sympathy towards interface difficulties and will nourish offers of assistance and flexibility. Synergy will also be apparent – the value of the whole will be greater than the sum of the values of the separate parts.

Group activities require careful planning and some control by a facilitator if they are to achieve the best outcome.

AREAS OF PARTICULAR CONCERN

Relationships with the risk facilitator and risk process manager

The risk process manager will be involved with the project team on a regular and ongoing basis. A risk facilitator will be involved as required to contribute particular skills to further the risk management process.

The term 'risk process manager' will be used in this section to refer to both the risk facilitator and the risk process manager.

In theory, the risk process manager is a 'neutral' influence on the behaviour of the individuals and team. His or her role is to elicit and capture data about risk in an impartial manner and to reflect information in a controlled and structured way. In reality, the risk process manager's relationship with the project team can have a major bearing on the outcome of the project risk management process. The project team will need to trust the risk process manager's judgement and take his or her guidance during the exercise. Four aspects of the relationship are worthy of note:

1   The project team will tend to distrust a risk process manager who does not have relevant domain knowledge. It is unlikely, for instance, that a risk process manager fundamentally trained in software engineering will be readily accepted by a team who are building a bridge.

2   Risk process managers may hold other authoritative positions (for example, project manager, QA manager or technical manager) which influence their actual or perceived impartiality. It can be difficult for risk process managers with conflicting responsibilities to create a clear boundary between their opinions and judgements and their relationship with the project team, particularly if some areas of risk arise from decisions that the risk manager has made in another authoritative capacity. The risk process manager may also be a line manager over staff involved in the project risk management process, and typical relationship patterns between them may influence the way in which the risk process manager views the information provided. Similarly, the providers of information may formulate their responses in the context of their long-term relationship with the risk process manager in his or her other roles.

3   The interpersonal skills of risk process managers – that is, their ability to develop sound and trusting relationships with individuals within the project – are crucial to the effective implementation of project risk management. Despite best endeavours, however, some relationships

never develop to this level of trust. Occasionally, the relationship is sufficiently poor as to be destructive. Chauvinism and racial prejudice are also not entirely unknown in the workplace.

4   Unless the risk process manager is an independent consultant, or otherwise unknown to the project team, a prior relationship may exist with some project staff arising from the risk process manager's previous positions. This historical relationship will affect the level of support and trust between the manager and the project team. Where risk process managers are provided by a central risk management group, the previous successes/failures of the group (and the esteem in which the group's manager is held) will tend to influence the way in which the project team treats the risk process manager.

It is important to appreciate that the complexities of a project staff's behaviour are not immune to the character and influence of the risk process manager. Every player (stakeholder) in the project risk management process will influence, in subtle or substantive ways, the behaviour of the other players. These influences may be slight in their impact on the outcome, but they will have some effect.

Risk transfer and allocation from customer to supplier

On the surface, transferring a risk down the supply chain from either customer or prime contractor can appear to be an ideal way of managing a risk; the risk is then perceived to be 'someone else's problem'. However, care must be taken, as the risk will probably impact on the original risk-owning organisation if its new owner doesn't manage it well.

For example, risks that impact on the overall project timescale and performance will affect the customer and the prime contractor as well as the supplier. In some instances, if the risk is critical to the overall achievement of the programme, then the prime contractor is likely to pay a much higher price than the supplier, due to project overhead costs, delayed milestone payments, and possible penalty clauses. The customer organisation may also suffer significantly if the project deliverables are seriously delayed or fail to meet the required performance. Often a delay in the arrival of deliverables can result in the customer having to keep existing assets and systems in use for longer, and this can require unplanned manpower and costs.

The acceptance of appropriate risk can be a good thing, as it can be seen to add value. For example, there are instances where it is most beneficial for the customer to hold the risk – say, where the probability of the risk is small, but the impact is unacceptably high. In these circumstances the most cost-effective solution for the whole supply chain is for the customer to ring-fence the risk, pay the full impact should the risk occur, but pay nothing if it doesn't.

Sometimes, the level of risk within a contract can be too great to make the contract viable. The wise contractor will recognise this and turn the work away, whereas the unwise contractor, in his overeagerness to win the contract, will rush into an unprofitable position that could seriously affect his credibility and reputation.

Conversely, the sharing of the positive impact of opportunities can help to ensure that they are realised, as all parties have a stake in their success.

Teamwork at enterprise level

In an ideal world, the problems inherent in risk transfer and allocation (and many others) can be solved by extending true teamwork across all the organisations involved in the project. Here, a single risk register is shared openly between all organisations, who work to the overall good of the project and its participating organisations, as would be found in a good partnership.

This ideal can be hard to achieve and has to be built on a strong foundation of trust between all participating organisations. The trust required can be difficult to build, particularly if the trust has been broken by one of the parties in previous situations.

If the required trust does not exist from the outset, then a useful way of facilitating a more trusting environment, is to agree a 'code of conduct' between the organisations. This brief document (one page of A4 should be adequate), will define the acceptable and unacceptable behaviours for all parties within the team, with respect to the shared data. For example, one statement on the code of conduct may well be: 'The information shared between the parties, shall not be shared outside the parties forming the project team, without first obtaining permission from the originating organisation for the relevant piece of information.'

Estimates and forecasting

Since the objective of risk analysis is to create a basis on which effective decisions are made, the information must be as reliable as possible and the sources of unreliability well understood. One of the main sources of unreliability comes from biases held by the specialist(s) providing the data. People tend to make judgements on a subset of the information available to them, reducing complex analysis to short-cut procedures to simplify the task of assessing the probability and impact of risks. This can lead to systematic biases and potentially costly errors in the decisions based on this information. Such biases may be due to one or more of the following common errors in the specialist's intuitive approach to information processing:

- Some properties of the available data may be overemphasised, leading to a higher or lower estimate of risk. This can be due to an overreliance on some characteristic of evidence and/or neglect of other evidence.
- The subjective probability given to a risk may be based on personal experience. However, this past experience may not be a valid sample of expected outcomes from similar risks on the current programme.

- Individual estimates tend to be generated by adjustment from an initial value – a process known to give rise to biases. In the cumulative case, the full impact of the multiple effect of a number of risks may not be considered if the estimate of individual risks is perceived to be low.
- The order in which risks are portrayed or viewed may impact on initial evaluations and estimations.

There are other behavioural tendencies that can give rise to inaccurate or unrealistic biases in an individual's estimate and which arise directly from the specific nature of the problem. In most cases, the individual is totally unaware that they introduce such bias and may defend their 'biased' estimates if challenged. These bias mechanisms include the following:

- An individual's level of concern over a risk may reduce in succeeding timeframes. Rather than acknowledge a bias in successive/preceding estimating, he or she may invent spurious 'causal' explanations.
- An individual's estimate of probabilities tends to be influenced by the units and scaling of the primary data. People tend to give more weight to data that is in the same units as the outcome.
- People tend to have a high opinion of their own predictive ability for single situations, leading to overconfidence in their own judgements.
- Typically, people tend to estimate conservatively for single judgements and overestimate the combined effects of cascading multi-stage problems.
- People tend to 'adjust' probability estimates in accordance with their perception of the personal rewards/repercussions that will result from the various uses of the assessment. Where there is a conflict of interest, estimates may be suspect.
- An expert in a particular field may suppress uncertainty for fear of seeming less than knowledgeable.

The risk process manager should first recognise that such biases exist and devise mechanisms to minimise or overcome these biases.

Conclusion

This chapter has set out a wide range of issues that collectively influence human behaviour and, in particular, behaviour towards risk in the project risk management environment. It has demonstrated not only the complexity that exists, but also some of the causes of behaviour which at times might appear unpredictable or which may differ from that expected. This is just the tip of the iceberg where behavioural issues are concerned. However armed with the knowledge imparted here and the techniques suggested, the risk facilitator and process manager should achieve greater understanding, consistency and objectivity, which can only be beneficial to the project risk management process.

7

The Application of PRAM

This chapter considers the choices to be made when applying risk management, taking into account factors such as the business priorities, organisational culture and risk maturity, nature of the project and risk capability of the project staff.

INTRODUCTION

Risk management makes sound sense in theory but, to be useful to a project, the theoretical benefits need to be realised. This can be a formidable task if not undertaken in the correct manner. The aim of this chapter is to provide practical advice on implementing risk management within an organisation or project and ensuring its long-term success.

It is worth noting that projects fail for many reasons, including ineffective management of risks. However, poor initial estimating and poor application of project management will also adversely affect the outcomes. It is important that risk management is not seen as a solution for these other problems but that it is used as a part of the portfolio of techniques to achieve a successful project outcome.

Although it may be easy to tell a project manager to apply risk management processes on his or her project, unless boundaries are provided and objectives defined it will not be easy either to measure success or demonstrate the value of the process. Therefore the benefits will vary according to the project manager's understanding of why risk management is being applied and what it should be producing. Successfully implementing risk management requires a consideration of the reasons for introducing it as well as of the level of commitment given to it.

As with any endeavour, then, defining the goals for the process is critical. To do this a risk manager must ask 'Why do we need to apply risk management?' and 'How should it be applied?'. As formal risk management processes cover a variety of different techniques, with different complexities, it is also essential that the correct process be applied to the different levels of the organisation.

To be effective, risk management must involve all levels of organisational responsibility and be applied continuously and consistently, constantly moving forwards as the projects and the business evolves. To ensure success, the organisation must require that the risk management process be treated with respect within the organisation and be implemented early to achieve the greatest benefit.

This chapter will therefore seek to describe the key decisions that need to be made and the hard and soft skills required when implementing risk management.

THE BUSINESS PERSPECTIVE

Although this *Guide* is about project risk management, it would be naive to ignore the business environment within which the project must operate. Whether the project is internal or carried out on behalf of a client, it still has a purpose for the organisation and the organisation will still have a responsibility for the project outcome. This responsibility will normally require senior management to understand and be involved in risk management. Furthermore, approval to undertake a project, or to bid for one, will almost certainly require senior-level authorisation. In light of this, it is normal business practice to construct a business case to inform senior management of all the arguments for and against the proposed project. Again, this would normally include an assessment of risks. In some organisations senior management also hold some or all of the contingency budget and / or management reserve and will only release the funds to the project when the risk management processes have appropriately justified this action.

There is no single guidance that will suit all organisations – at the business level organisations tend to operate according to their own characteristics. It is also inappropriate to state 'best practice' because, again, the needs and the nature of the business determine what is 'best' for this community. There are, however, a number of common themes which can be explored.

The business case

Prior to a project being authorised, decisions are made to organise, structure, resource, locate, manage and share the tasks in order to manage exposure to risk. Where the project is subject to competition, these decisions may be made by the sales and marketing department in order to improve the competitive position. Decisions that inspire customer confidence, minimise the contingency or management reserve in the selling price, or reduce the chance of failure, are usually made on the basis of reducing risk. Potential internal projects are similarly subjected to the same type of arguments, but perhaps in this case from the department manager. Whereas 'risk' is commonly used to justify vagueness in project plans, it is less common for that risk to be clearly identified or qualified or for mitigation action to be tested against alternatives. Employing formal risk management, even at this pre-approval stage in the project life cycle, enables the development of better strategies and a far more robust justification for the project. Improving the strategies reduces the likelihood of downstream failures. The causes and effects of risks and strategies can be described in the business plan.

The risk management process described in Chapter 4 includes an initial iteration of risk management to inform the development of appropriate business strategies. As recommended in this *Guide*, the risk process must be carried out in respect of the project's stated objectives. For the business case these would be business objectives, and these may be quite different from the objectives for the eventual project. For instance, a business objective may be to secure a position in the marketplace, support a company investment programme, retain a facility or reinforce a relationship with a strategic partner. The assessment of risks to these objectives would give rise to the development of response strategies, and these would be used to set the detailed objectives for the project tasks. Risk management would then be used to assess risks to this project's objectives.

Where appropriate, the funds required to cover the cost of each agreed risk response should be identified. This process should be used to encourage risk owners to identify the most appropriate response and to gain the best value for money when managing the risk.

Business commonality

Whilst each project manager must decide the most appropriate means for addressing risk, there are potential benefits of scale in taking a largely common approach throughout the business enterprise. Using a common framework and templates, the same high-level processes and the same tools and systems provides a sound basis for training staff, reduces the investment in different (or even home-grown) tools and supports the mobility of expertise between projects. For this reason there is a sound argument for the business to appoint a 'champion' to provide the corporate vision for risk management and to determine the common standards, policies and practices that the organisation will apply throughout its projects. The approach may be different for projects of different natures – for instance, with different sizes or levels of complexity – but even these differences may be accommodated within a broadly common approach.

Each organisation will have unique circumstances that drive its decisions, but there are some simple rules to help with the effectiveness of taking a common approach:

1 **Involve the user community**. The corporate entity should not allow a single individual (or small team) to make policy decisions and then attempt to sell them to the users. All senior stakeholders (including project managers) should be involved in the decision-making process in accordance with clear objectives set by the senior management.

2 **Align to the quality management system (QMS).** Risk management should be treated like other business processes; it should be aligned with the quality standards and be issued as part of the QMS. In particular, the risk management processes should be aligned and be coherent with other business processes that include a risk element.

3 **Conform to IT policies**. Risk management tools should be selected in accordance with the corporate approach to software applications. Many organisations do not support the development of home-grown applications (even simple databases), and some more sophisticated tools require annual maintenance costs that must be included within the IT department's long-term budgets. Furthermore, there are often efficiency gains if tools are integrated with other applications.

INTRODUCING RISK MANAGEMENT INTO AN ORGANISATION

Common sense plays a key role in the choice of techniques to be used. Never underestimate the ability to intuitively know the right technique for a project. However, the project culture must also be considered when choosing techniques to ensure that the approach taken is appropriate to the intended audience's maturity. An understanding of the client organisation's attitude to risk and the message it sends to those working with risk is crucial. Is there a mechanism for rewarding good risk management or sharing the benefits? Do colleagues or team members work well together and support one another in achieving success?

Choosing projects for implementing risk management

Often an organisation will decide to implement risk management principles because a project is already out of control, or will enforce it on every project irrespective of the expectation of risk or readiness of the project team to accept the principles. These are both less than ideal approaches. The greatest benefits of the risk management process are realised when it is implemented at the earliest possible stage in a project and continued throughout its life cycle. The techniques can then be introduced without any false expectations being attached to them, and the project team can learn how to use them as the project develops. Having learnt from this experience, project staff can apply risk management more effectively on the next project.

Because it concerns understanding what can go wrong and what opportunities exist, risk management should be implemented on projects which have a clear objective. Without knowing what the objectives are, it is difficult to understand specific risks and what the project team can do to overcome the uncertainty. Successful implementation of risk management also depends on a competent team that is focused on delivering the project objectives. Only then can appropriate risks and, more importantly, appropriate control measures be identified.

Setting objectives

For the implementation of risk management to be successful on a project it is necessary to define the objectives of the process. The initial question should be: 'Why do we need risk management?' If the answer is 'Because we must meet specific project constraints', then critical success factors based on project constraints should form the starting point.

Although sometimes a mandated client requirement will be the initial reason for undertaking risk management, there are other reasons why risk management should be undertaken. However, the benefits achieved from the process will vary according to the project manager's understanding of why risk management is being applied and what process is to be applied. The successful implementation of risk management requires, in particular, a thorough consideration of the reasons for introducing it and the level of commitment to be applied. Clarity of intention during the initial stages of implementation will lead to better results.

Risk management must be defined within the context of its application. If the process is to be applied to a project or programme then the life cycle or stage of the project must be considered. If a project is still within the bid or tender stages, risk management may be applied to enhance the project team's understanding of a developing budget or schedule, through the quantification of risks. If risk management is to support the ongoing development phase of a project, it is used to support the reduction and management of risk in order to meet specific constraints.

It may be beneficial to take a top-down approach to the setting of the process objectives and allow the high-level output requirement of the process to define the nature and extent of the process and techniques to be applied. In other words, asking the initial question 'Why do we need risk management?' helps define the techniques and process steps that meet the specific project requirements. It is important, though, to apply these steps continuously and consistently, constantly moving forwards as the project or business evolves to ensure that new reasons for undertaking risk management are understood and addressed.

Measuring success

As the project progresses, the reassessment of risks creates a risk trend that can provide effective monitoring and control of the project risks. Reassessment highlights not only those risks that are under control but also, and more importantly, those risks that are not being controlled by the dedicated action plans. This plays a valuable part in ensuring that the right actions are in place to effectively control identified project risks.

Risk reviews should be used to determine the success of risk management. They should be designed to ensure that ongoing risk mitigation and control are appropriate and effective. To ensure that risk mitigation is appropriate, it is necessary to review the risk assessment data and identify any new risks.

To ensure that risk control is effective, it is necessary to review the aims and objectives of risk response actions and verify that they are being implemented as planned.

As a project progresses, risks evolve and new risks may be identified. The status of project risks should therefore be under continuous review. In an environment characterised by a good risk management culture, risk management will be interwoven with other project management processes so that a risk can be reviewed as and when necessary. However, experience shows that a project should also have a planned risk review schedule guaranteeing that all risks are reviewed on a regular basis. The frequency of risk reviews should be designed to optimise the cost-effectiveness of the risk management process.

For companies wishing to improve performance the best practice is to measure the progress being made against specific metrics for risk management. These might include occurrence of non-forecasted risks, impacts different from those forecast and cost-effectiveness of the treatment of risk across the whole company. As with all such measurement, the cost-value and utility of measurements must be carefully considered. This applies particularly to risk management where the dynamics of probability and the relationship between handling and impacts make the results of measurement subject to interpretation. It is also clear that capturing and tracking these types of measurement will be time-consuming and often difficult.

Understanding the organisation's risk management maturity

Before any journey can be made, or destination reached, a starting point must be identified. Likewise, risk management on a project cannot successfully be implemented if the project team or organisation does not know whether it has the skills or the understanding that are required to put it into practice. An organisation can have the best process on paper, but if the team cannot apply it the process will fail.

A necessary step is to determine the project team's current capability or risk maturity in order to ensure that the right skills are in place to make the process a success. The method to determine this capability is often known as a risk maturity assessment. Such an assessment allows the organisation to question its key stakeholders' understanding of the principles of risk management, makes stakeholders aware of the organisation's approach to risk and checks that they have the necessary skills and resources to complete the task. A revealed lack of risk maturity in an organisation highlights the need to educate staff in risk management prior to applying it on a project.

Using the business process

To enable everyone to understand why risk management is being implemented, what it is and what is expected from it, it is useful to develop a project risk strategy document and procedures or guidelines. The risk strategy should be included in the risk management plan and define the broad steps to be taken by the project to manage risks (perhaps as a specific study). The risk procedures or guidelines will support the expectation that everyone has the same level of understanding of the approach to be used. If they are well communicated, they prevent misunderstandings, as the information transferred will be factual rather than hearsay. Because they also underpin a commonality of approach, procedures or guidelines complement the need to learn from experience; at the end of a project, the information produced from the risk management process can be stored alongside information from other projects, thus building up a historical database for the benefit of future projects and the education of new members of staff. As the generic risk management process must imperatively be tailored to each project, the procedure should emphasise the unique features of the process that make it project-specific.

Starting simple

When first introducing risk management, it may be necessary to select simple and easily understandable techniques for each phase of the process to ensure that they can be implemented with the minimum of difficulty. This will also help project managers understand how useful the process can be. This may not be the ideal situation for the organisation, but it goes a long way to ensuring the initial acceptance of risk management. Once these initial techniques have been understood and put into practice, more complex techniques may be introduced. Experience shows that once project managers have seen the initial benefits of introducing risk management they are keen to improve the processes and refine their use of the techniques to gain the maximum benefits available. Gaining the support of project managers and/or sponsors will underpin the implementation of risk management on the project and can greatly contribute towards the successful application of the process.

It is also essential to try to keep the information at a usable level. As risk information can be open to differing interpretations, it is helpful to record risks in a consistent manner to avoid the risk being misconstrued. This often means keeping risk descriptions short and to the point; some organisations use the 'if' ... 'then' format for their descriptions, thus breaking them down into the definitions of cause and consequence. Similarly, when assessing risks it is critical to develop assessment criteria which are realistic in terms of the risk impact that the project can accept.

Using an appropriate level of formality

Whilst the methodology applied to risk management may be common throughout the organisation, it is unlikely that a common level of implementation will be required (as illustrated in Figure 7.1a). Projects tend to be of different sizes (for example, from a single installation to a worldwide

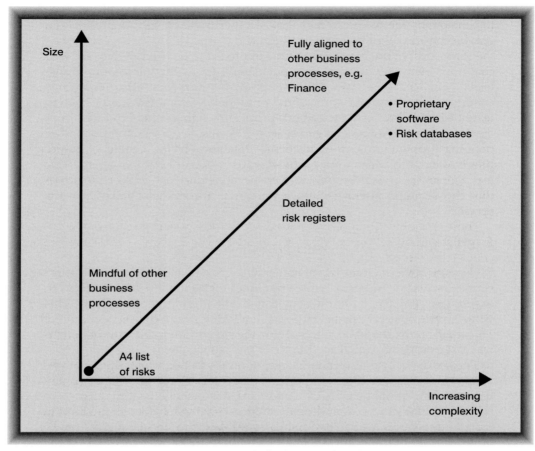

Figure 7.1a *Level of risk process formality*

installation involving many hundreds of sites) and varying degrees of complexity (for example, ranging from a minor modification to an existing product to the development of a new product using a new technology). For a small low-complexity project a simple risk register might be satisfactory whilst for a large, complex, multi-company, multinational project a web-based fully integrated risk environment might be more appropriate.

Choosing techniques

There are many risk management techniques that can be used to support and drive the risk management process, and these are outlined in Chapter 8 and detailed in the Appendix. Techniques selected for a project should be tailored to the information needed by that project; in addition, the size and nature of the project, the time available for the study, the information available, the project culture and the experience or risk maturity of the staff should also be considered.

A fundamental decision in terms of the breadth of the process employed relates to the use of qualitative or quantitative analysis and assessment. The starting point for the risk process and its successful implementation is to ensure that a consistent evaluation and prioritisation of the risks is undertaken. This will focus management attention on those risks that are most significant to the success of the project. A consistent approach depends on defining a common basis for determining risk probability and impact. Key to this is the use of qualitative techniques, commonly known as qualitative assessment, involving the development of assessment criteria or narratives that define the different likelihood and impact levels associated with the project.

These assessment criteria can be developed for any size or scope of project. In general they reflect a range of boundary values that can be used to consistently assess different perceptions of risk significance.

Occasionally, the assessment of a risk's likelihood and impact may need to be further developed to provide more precise values. This technique is often known as quantitative analysis and involves redefining the likelihood and impact of a risk to provide more of a numerical value – for example, a percentage probability of occurrence and impacts defined in terms of numerical cost or schedule implications.

Depending on the risk maturity of the project team and the resources committed to risk management, it may not be possible to carry out full quantitative risk analyses on every project. The information gained from the earlier qualitative risk analysis techniques is often used to prioritise risks in the first stages. A quantitative risk analysis can then be carried out on the more critical risks in order to gain a better understanding of them.

Timescales for the completion of a risk management exercise also have a significant influence on the techniques used. Brainstorming and structured interviews are relatively quick to complete, can provide a significant amount of information and are therefore ideal when time is short. It should also be remembered that the full participation of the project manager in the initial phases of using such techniques can send a clear message to staff that there is commitment to the success of risk management.

Defining deliverables

Chapter 5 has already introduced the various documented outputs of the risk management process.

The initial risk management deliverable for almost every project is the risk management plan (RMP). The RMP is prepared to document the risk management process to be implemented by the project team in support of the management of risk on the project. The document identifies the procedures that the team will apply to identify, assess, manage and control project risks. It describes the process whereby risks (threats and opportunities) that could affect the project are identified and assessed, analyses their impact on project timescales and costs, and implements the appropriate management control to minimise the impacts of those risks on the successful completion of the project. It covers the identification, assessment, analysis, management and control of risk and, as such, provides a basis for defining the risk management responsibilities of the key stakeholders as far as they relate to the risk management process, as well as a basis for defining the risk management roles and responsibilities of each team member. The document can also list the risk management software tools and techniques to be used to support the risk process and how the process will be integrated into the project management culture.

To support the risk process, the risks and their meaning must be clearly visible. The documentation should clearly identify ownership of risk and monitor the trend of risk exposure over the duration of the project. Typical risk management documents will include the overall risk register and periodic risk management status reports.

Risks identified during the course of the project execution are often recorded within a risk management system that enables easy updating of the risks and is capable of producing the risk management documentation, including the risk register. The risk register is a result of the risk assessment undertaken by the project team, and its overall purpose is to present a statement of the risks and their subsequent management actions for the course of the project. It serves a number of functions: not only does it identify risks, their timing and their likely impact on the project; but by recording the results of the risk assessment process and the supporting discussions relating to the risks, it also provides a basis for management risk reviews.

A risk status report is often developed to provide the senior management team with a periodic overview of the health of the risk management process. The report covers risks raised during the period as well as those risks which have been closed and the reasons why. It also details the status of risk management responses, outlining those responses that have been activated (either successfully or unsuccessfully) and those that are delayed or have been missed.

Learning from experience and evolving processes

It is common for the risk management process to evolve over time. As mentioned previously, the initial enthusiasm for risk management often reduces as more and more live issues take priority over discussing things that may happen in the future. There are several ways to overcome this tendency, such as reviewing key risks relevant to the current stage, reviewing the top five high priority risks in a given category or reviewing supplier risks before awarding a contract. By using these strategies the process evolves to suit the changing nature of the project and the team is encouraged to maintain a degree of interest.

The risk management process should also provide an audit trail. Therefore as changes occur it is important to capture them and maintain a historic record and reasons for change. This aids the process of learning from experience and builds a knowledge database that can be used when faced with similar risks. A large part of the learning from experience is captured by recording and evidencing the reasons for closing risks down.

MAINTAINING INTEREST

All levels of the organisation should be encouraged to become involved in the risk process. Highlighting the benefits of involvement is key, and this means naming successful individuals in board meetings, management team reviews and in reports, and rewarding positive input to the risk management process. Leading from the top is also very important. The board needs to be involved in the risk management process especially in the light of recent internal control requirements which state that the board must be aware of the risks to their business.

The successful management of risks involves the whole project team. To this end, information on project risks should be made available to everyone and each should be encouraged to make a contribution although without undermining the specific responsibility of the risk owner.

Training and awareness

Gaining contribution and ongoing commitment is critical to the success of the risk management process. A forum or framework should be put in place to highlight the importance and increase the visibility of risk management within the organisation and project. This can be achieved in a number of ways. First, a statement on risk can be included in the organisation's dispatches or newsletter. This emphasises that risk management is taken seriously and is a newsworthy item. The use of web technologies and company intranets is also becoming common practice. This medium may be used to provide information on risk management best practice, and the benefits and progress achieved to date. It can include details of management techniques, a facility for giving feedback to the risk team or champion, explanations for the application of risk management and lessons learnt from risk management in other project areas.

One reason for not pursuing such a process is usually the lack of understanding within an organisation. Specific risk awareness processes can help remedy this shortcoming. Many organisations run induction courses for new employees on topics such as company procedures, roles and responsibilities and project and quality management, and risk management awareness training could usefully be added to their new employee training. Improvement in risk management commitment and contribution within an organisation can also often be achieved by introducing very brief risk awareness seminars and formal training for key project members.

CONCLUSION

This chapter has explained why the application of risk management within a particular enterprise needs to be considered fully and with a sensitive appreciation of the specific nature of that organisation and its projects before changes are implemented. It has provided guidance and insight into how this might best be achieved and on the implications of the decisions made. It is hoped that this advice, together with the guidance in other sections of this *Guide*, will give the reader sufficient confidence to embark on a programme of activities to implement formal risk management. It should be recognised, however, that the process of change, such as the introduction of formal risk management, is almost always a longer and more complex issue than first envisaged. The practical realisation of sound risk management will be a hard-won battle, but one that is worth the fight.

8

Tools and Techniques

This chapter gives an overview of the wide choice of tools and techniques that are available to assist in undertaking the risk management process. The techniques are methods of carrying out particular elements of the risk management cycle that have proved to be effective when previously employed on projects. The tools are generic software products that can be employed by a project team to make efficient use of one or more of the risk management techniques.

Following a short section outlining the issues involved when selecting tools and techniques for the risk management process, each of the key elements of the risk management cycle is taken in turn and the appropriate techniques for that element are identified. The application of each technique is described briefly and is accompanied by notes that discuss its merits and limitations. Having chosen a combination of risk management techniques, a project team will then need to turn its attention to the selection of tools that facilitate their use. The final sections of this chapter therefore identify the different types of tool that are available and describe the features that make them suitable for use.

For more information, readers can refer to the Appendix, which describes the implementation of some of the more commonly practised techniques. Readers who would like further information provided by tools suppliers can access the APM Risk SIG risk tools document via the APM's website at www.apm.org.uk.

SELECTING TOOLS AND TECHNIQUES

When focusing their risk management process, project teams should choose the combination of tools and techniques that is most appropriate to their circumstances. The following notes provide guidance on the issues involved, and the summary tables at the end of the chapter provide additional support.

1   The selected techniques should encompass all the key elements of the risk management cycle from risk identification through to the implementation

of risk management actions. For example, there is little point in adopting sophisticated risk assessment techniques unless the risk identification and risk response processes are also sound.

2   Some techniques are suitable for risk management in the earliest phases of a project (including pre-project approval), whilst others are more applicable to later phases.

3   Employing any risk management technique costs time and money, so its use should be justified by the potential benefits.

4   When selecting techniques the project team should bear in mind the benefits it is aiming to deliver through its risk management process. Techniques conducive to openness of communication are likely to be successful in achieving both hard and soft benefits.

5   Where qualitative and quantitative assessment techniques are used, risk management should be an internally coherent process, and project teams should ensure that there are connections between the two.

6   Risk management should also be integrated with other project disciplines, particularly those associated with leadership, planning and review. Techniques that are complementary to such disciplines are more likely than others to succeed.

RISK IDENTIFICATION TECHNIQUES

Assumptions and constraints analysis

Project definition and planning processes inevitably make use of a large number of assumptions. If these assumptions are recorded, they can be used to identify threats by assessing the probability that each assumption will be met and the impact on the project should the assumption be violated. Constraints can be assessed in a similar manner. In cases where there is a significant probability that a constraint could be relaxed or disregarded, opportunities may be identifiable.

Checklists

A checklist is a detailed *aide-mémoire* for the identification of potential risks. Checklists are usually generated by organisations to reflect the key issues that affect their environment. They are a useful means of preserving the lessons learnt from the occurrence of previous events and they can be incorporated into self-assessment processes or used as a safety net for reviews. However, projects frequently find themselves breaking new ground, so checklists should be used in combination with other more proactive risk identification techniques.

A weakness of checklists is that they can become either too exhaustive or too project-specific to be of practical use. The lists need to be managed to ensure that they gather lessons learned from previous projects in a format that is useful to ongoing and future projects.

Prompt lists

A prompt list is another form of risk identification *aide-mémoire*, but one that uses headings, usually related to generic sources of risks. The aim of a prompt list is to stimulate proactive and lateral thinking. Prompt lists are therefore a resource that can be used to support other techniques, such as brainstorming. They can also be included in plans or procedures to indicate the breadth of issues that risk management is concerned with. Prompt lists may be structured as a generic risk breakdown structure (see p. 100).

Brainstorming

Brainstorming captures risks quickly, and offers a means of raising enthusiasm for risk management across a team. It can also be used to engage project stakeholders in the risk identification process. An independent facilitator is normally used to ensure that the session is sufficiently well structured and maintains a good pace. Typically the output of a brainstorm is a list of risks, each described by a phrase or sentence indicative of the risk source.

Although widely used by projects, brainstorming sessions do have some limitations. Despite rules designed to encourage equality amongst the participants, the nature of the event can result in bias in favour of the extrovert. This is an issue over which the facilitator has to maintain control. It should also be made clear to the team that a brainstorming session does not mark the only opportunity for individuals to raise risks. As a project progresses, risks evolve and new risks emerge. Risk identification should be a continuous process, and, if this is not recognised, the output from a brainstorming session can dominate the risk register at the expense of new risks.

Interviews

Interviews are often used for risk identification when it is not practicable to commit a team to a single meeting. Interviews have many of the advantages of brainstorming and require a similar semi-structured approach, with the interviewer assuming the facilitator's role. The disadvantages are that the process consumes more of the facilitator's time and that opportunities afforded by the cross-fertilisation of ideas are more limited. However, some people are more comfortable with expressing themselves openly in a one-to-one situation, particularly if the interviewer is perceived to be independent.

Interviews can also be employed for risk assessment and the management of risk responses. However, interviews used for these purposes will be more structured. When interviews are used regularly, it may be convenient to use them to encompass all key elements of the risk management cycle. This generates a regular opportunity for the identification of new risks.

Strengths, Weaknesses, Opportunities and Threats (SWOT) analysis

SWOT analysis comprises a breakdown of the strengths and weaknesses inherent in a project's circumstances that give rise to opportunities and threats – that is, expose it to risk. SWOT may also be useful in risk planning by considering how the strengths and opportunities can be used to reduce the weaknesses and threats. A key advantage of using this technique may be that the project's organisation already uses it for the dissemination of issues associated with other functions such as marketing and business development. Its use would therefore be consistent with integrating the risk management process with such functions, many of which are associated with activities in the earlier phases of projects.

Stakeholder analysis

Stakeholder analysis concerns the desirability of the objectives and key features of the project as perceived by each stakeholder. Risks may be identified where requirements are found to be in conflict. In a wide-ranging stakeholder analysis, stakeholders may include the customer, project teams, senior management, corporate management, subcontractors, operators, consumers, political organisations and the general public.

An important advantage of stakeholder analysis is that it can be applied to projects during their earlier phases. It can therefore be used to integrate risk management with the project management processes that produce statements of requirement.

Project monitoring

A project team might employ a variety of ways to monitor project progress. Progress reviews offer the opportunity for the identification of emerging risks, particularly on issues related to cost and schedule. The inclusion of risk as an agenda item for progress reviews can be a useful discipline and helps to integrate risk management with other project management strategies. If the project utilises earned value techniques, then the cost performance and schedule performance indices (CPIs and SPIs) are useful early indicators of emerging risk.

Nominal group technique (NGT)

NGT is a development of the standard brainstorming technique that is designed to offset the threat of group dominance by individuals. Participants are asked to record their perceptions of risk privately. The facilitator then asks each of the group, in turn, to nominate a unique risk. In this way, everyone has to contribute and the potential for intimidation is reduced. The technique can also lead into the process of risk assessment if, having derived a risk list, the group members are then asked to score each risk.

Delphi technique

The Delphi technique originated at the Rand Corporation as a means of predicting consequences of then-current policy decisions. The technique may be used for risk identification or assessment and operates by using a qualified group to gather and respond to opinion. An advantage is that it can be carried out remotely and/or anonymously – for example, by e-mail. This overcomes some of the logistical and group dynamics limitations of brainstorming, whilst retaining at least some scope for the exchange of ideas. However, the Delphi technique can be quite time consuming. Consequently, experience shows that too many rounds of data gathering can result in a high drop-out rate.

Technology readiness levels (TRLs)

Technology readiness levels (TRLs) are an approach to the assessment of technological maturity developed by NASA and increasingly adopted by other industries working in an environment of rapid technological change. A project's technical solution can be assessed for its exposure to risk by determining the TRL for each system and subsystem. System components characterised by a relatively low TRL and an uncertain maturation plan can be identified as technology risks.

Peer review

It may be useful to engage an independent expert to review project plans and risks, particularly if the risk assessment founded on the identified risks is to be provided as evidence at a major project decision point. Peer review may also help to provide a final check for consistency in the risk identification process. However, care should be taken to involve the relevant team members so that peer review is not perceived to be a barrier to the aims of open communication.

Capitalising on a good risk management culture

A risk management culture embraces risk awareness and the willingness of all personnel to play an active role in risk-related processes. A good risk management culture is characterised by openness of communication, learning rather than blaming and a determination to tackle risks at source. One benefit of having such a culture is that risk-aware project personnel become accustomed to identifying risks as and when they become apparent. This is likely to achieve better results than any technique that relies on a planned activity, since risk reduction action is generally at its most effective when applied at the earliest opportunity.

QUALITATIVE AND QUANTITATIVE RISK ASSESSMENT

When focusing risk management, a project team should understand its purposes in carrying out risk assessment. If the main purpose of the risk management process is to add value by implementing actions proactively in response to risks, then the techniques for risk assessment should reflect the management realities of implementing actions. These include the following:

- Actions that address risk at source tend to be those that are the most effective.
- Secondary consequences of risk impact are often underestimated.
- Risks are more likely to be acted on if responsibility is allocated to individuals.
- Management time and budgeting dictate that actions have to be prioritised.

These practical realities set the agenda for qualitative risk assessment techniques.

Project stakeholders may also require that risk assessment be used for the production of risk-based forecasts of outcome variance or to support specific decisions with a quantitative analysis. If so, the project will select quantitative risk analysis techniques designed to address the questions posed. Many of the quantitative techniques described in this chapter also have the advantage of combining information on risks and uncertainties in a manner that models the overall risk to the project. In doing so, they provide different approaches to the identification of sources of project risk that overcome the limitation of analysis based on individual risks.

QUALITATIVE RISK ASSESSMENT TECHNIQUES

Probability assessment

Probability is usually one of the two dimensions used to assess the size or importance of a risk (the other dimension being impact). The risk probability is the estimated likelihood of the risk event occurring and is typically recorded as a percentage or as a range (for example, 20–50 per cent) denoted by a word indicating its significance (for example, 'medium'). In cases where risks are associated with events that are more or less inevitable, a project could choose to use 'frequency of occurrence' as an alternative measure to probability.

In some applications of risk management it is recommended that threats with a high probability (say, over 50 per cent) are managed as issues on the assumption that they will occur. The reciprocal probability that they will not occur is acknowledged as an opportunity. In other applications, the simpler approach of allowing risks to have higher probabilities (say, up to 90 per cent) is adopted. Yet another approach is to allow events with an estimated probability of 100 per cent to be also managed as risks, but only if there is a significant variance in their outcome. However, all risk management processes assume that problems or non-compliances in which there is little or no uncertainty will be treated as issues rather than risks.

Impact assessment

Risk impact is an assessment of the consequences to the project's objectives should the risk occur. It is common practice to assess impact against several different categories. On projects the risk impact categories will include timescale, cost and product, but they may also include other types of consequence such as commercial reputation, revenue, effect on operations and safety. Risk records often include a classification of risks by impact bands (for example, high, medium, low). In order to produce this data a project team has to define a classification rule set (risk criteria) for each impact type that is relevant.

The word 'impact' may be used to refer to either the adverse consequences of a threat-related risk or to the beneficial consequences of an opportunity. However, some users prefer to reserve the word 'impact' for threats and use the word 'benefit' to describe the consequence of an opportunity.

Risk descriptions/meta-language

Effective risk management requires that the source of each significant risk be understood in a way that facilitates the identification of proactive responses. Carefully structured and well-thought out risk descriptions can provide an important contribution to this aim. Typically, risk descriptions should include a statement of the underlying circumstances that expose the project to risk, the factors that could make a difference to whether the risk occurs and, should it occur, the extent of risk impact/benefit, and, finally, a description of the consequences. Risk meta-language provides a structure with which these elements of a risk description can be linked.

Influence diagrams

The occurrence of a risk often has a number of secondary effects. The use of influence diagrams can often help to identify these, thus leading to a more complete assessment of risk impact. They may also be useful for understanding the risk source, thus leading to the development of effective mitigation action. Using techniques like influence diagrams to trace back the source of risks is sometimes referred to as root cause analysis.

Influence diagrams can also form the structure for quantitative risk models in which the risk associated with a project target (for example, price or productivity) is analysed as the consequence of a number of input variables. Such models can detect the key influences on project outcome and allow the effects of uncertainty to be determined. The discipline of systems dynamics uses techniques such as this and, although a fuller explanation of systems dynamics is outside the scope of this *Guide*, the potential for its deployment within a risk management process should not be discounted.

Risk breakdown structures

A source-oriented risk breakdown structure is an hierarchical approach that recognises that risks can be identified and assessed at a number of levels. Assessment of a higher-level or generic risk may show that factors that influence its probability of occurrence, and the extent of its consequences may themselves be managed as discrete risks. These lower-level risks might then be broken down further in order to improve the focus of actions designed to control them. Organising risks in a hierarchy that recognises these relationships may have a number of advantages. One of the chief benefits is that it encourages a project team to understand the nature of its risks and the common threads that they have. Risk breakdown structures can also provide a useful tool for risk identification and a structure for risk ownership, leading to effective management of project risk at a strategic level as well as the management of individual risk events.

Probability-impact (P-I) matrices

P-I matrices are a technique used for the ranking of risks in order of significance. The assessments made for risk impact and probability are each determined against a scale whose increments are tailored to the project's size and environment. Typically, such scales are divided into five ranges labelled 'very high' to 'very low', or three ranges labelled 'high' to 'low'. Depending on its position on the P-I matrix, a risk can then be compared to others and ranked in order of significance.

There are a number of different ranking schemes for the cells in a P-I matrix. Most schemes are weighted towards impact rather than probability. Thus a low-probability/high-impact risk would be ranked above a risk that had a high probability but a low impact. However, there may also be projects for which the reverse would be more appropriate. The degree to which impact is weighted also varies. For example, if impact on safety is a key risk issue, there might be a relatively large bias towards impact. The P-I parameters and ranking scheme should therefore be project-specific and agreed between all stakeholders before risk assessment commences.

Risk improvement potential

Risk improvement potential is an assessment of the extent to which the probability, impact or the impact window of a risk can be changed. Risk improvement potential is usually expressed as high, medium or low. The purpose of risk improvement potential is to direct risk management effort cost-effectively. For example, a risk with high impact and medium probability would rank high on a P-I scale for attention. However, if its improvement potential is low, it would be given a lower priority than a risk with the same P-I score but a higher improvement potential.

There may also be merit in taking into account low improvement potential when reviewing risks at project approval decision points. If threats with high impact and high probability have low improvement potential then the project's feasibility may need to be reviewed unless a strategic approach to risk reduction is possible.

Risk impact windows and bubble diagrams

Bubble diagrams are a graphical technique for illustrating risk prioritisation. Risks are plotted on a graph as bubbles, whose areas (or colours) illustrate the estimated size of impact. The x-axis shows the time at which the risk could start to impact (the start of the risk impact window) and the y-axis shows risk probability. The format is designed to combine the probability and impact dimensions with that of time, and the viewer's attention is drawn to high-impact risks towards the top left-hand corner of the graph.

The weakness of this approach (and with the use of risk impact window approaches to risk prioritisation in general) is that, in many cases, the opportunity to manage a risk proactively may pass a long time before the start of the impact window. For example, the best opportunity to manage a risk that impacts on the integration of a complex system could occur during the system design stage. It may therefore be preferable to use the alternative approach of identifying windows of opportunity for management.

Expected value

An expected value is the best estimate of what should happen on average (that is, the mean outcome for cost, activity duration and so on). The expected value for a probability distribution function is calculated by multiplying all possible values by their probabilities. Expected values may be cumulative, particularly in the case of costs, but there may be factors involved that prevent this from being the case. For example, there may be overlaps or omissions inherent to the probability distributions being summed.

Risk register

A risk register provides a standard format in which to record risk information. As a minimum for each risk this information is likely to include the description, causes, probability, impact, mitigation actions, fallbacks, status and the names of individuals with responsibility for the risk's management. Depending on the risk management techniques selected, other data are also likely to be maintained, as appropriate.

Although a risk register can be maintained manually, most risk practitioners are likely to use a risk database tool for this purpose. Such tools may be designed for a stand-alone PC or designed for concurrent use by users linked through a network. Advice on selecting database tools is contained in the risk database tools section later in this chapter.

Project roll-up indicators (black/gold flags and traffic lights)

For project environments in which the users of risk information work at different points in the management hierarchy, a system may be required that combines risks in order to summarise them at the higher levels. This can be achieved by introducing a breakdown structure to the risk register by using parent–child relationships to show which risks should be combined at the higher levels. Processes that roll up risks into summarised form often include traffic light indicators (red = high risk, amber = medium risk and so on) that can be tailored to individual responsibility thresholds. Black flags are used in a similar way and denote groups of risks that, collectively, result in a high threat. Likewise, gold flags are used for groups of risks that result in a high opportunity.

QUANTITATIVE RISK ASSESSMENT TECHNIQUES

Probability distribution functions and three-point estimates

Many quantitative risk analysis techniques require probability distributions to be defined for the input parameters such as activity duration, cost, resource availability, risk impact and so on. Probability distribution functions can be continuous (for example, uniform, triangular, Beta PERT) or discrete (to represent alternative possible outcomes).

The uncertainty associated with non-uniform continuous probability distributions is often represented by three-point estimates (optimistic, most likely and pessimistic values). The estimate of these three points for each parameter in a quantitative model is therefore an important factor in achieving an accurate and reliable analysis.

Since the scenarios that correspond to the optimistic and pessimistic estimates may be significantly different to that which underlies the most likely value, good three-point estimates require an estimating strategy that is based on contingent thinking. The three-point estimating process can therefore often contribute to a deeper understanding of uncertainties and risks. In contrast, three-point estimates derived by an arbitrary plus/minus percentage around a planned value are often the source of poor quality input data for quantitative risk models.

First-pass (minimalist) quantitative models

First-pass quantitative models should be designed to identify which aspects of the project have the greatest influence on the overall project risk. This will focus further detailed assessment on areas of the project that will make the most difference if proactively managed. A minimalist approach to first-pass models may be constructed with simple probabilistic calculations concerning the uncertainties associated with key project drivers. This can make the first cycle of the risk process relatively short, whilst identifying a structure for more complex models requiring techniques such as Monte Carlo analysis.

Monte Carlo analysis

Monte Carlo analysis is a widely practised technique for quantitative risk analysis. For projects, the most common subjects for such analysis are the overall project cost and timescale. Single values for activity duration and cost are replaced by distributions based on estimations of uncertainty. The Monte Carlo process then simulates the project with multiple iterations to determine the probability distribution for the outcome cost or duration of the overall project or the achievement of a milestone. Data from Monte Carlo results can also be used to focus management attention on key programme risk issues.

Monte Carlo analysis is a powerful technique, but it does demand careful preparatory work. The quality of input data is critical to the reliability of the results. Construction of the project risk model and the collection of realistic risk estimates are activities that require experience, time and (if the results drive major decisions) the involvement of an independent party. A project should not expect to develop a detailed Monte Carlo risk model on its first pass of the risk process.

Correlation/statistical dependencies

When creating risk models, it is necessary to recognise that, in practice, there will be correlation between activity outcomes. In most cases there is a positive correlation, so that if some activities cost more or take longer than expected others will also tend to do so. Likewise, activities whose outcome is more favourable than expected often indicate a tendency for other activities to follow suit. Causes of this phenomenon include features of the project that are common to all activities (such as a common resource pool), detailed inter-relationships between activities that cannot be explicitly modelled and the effects of secondary risks (risks triggered by the occurrence of other risks).

Failure to simulate correlation between activities in risk models leads to analysis results that forecast an unrealistically low variance in outcome. Selection of the quantitative risk analysis tools should therefore take into account the ways in which correlation (or statistical dependencies) will be simulated.

Pre- and post-response assessments of probability and impact

A project may maintain assessments of probability and impact for the evaluation of risks both pre- and post-response. The pre-response assessment is based on a scenario in which the risk is accepted, and thus no specific response is made to reduce its effects. The post-response assessment is made to estimate the risk's effects based on a scenario in which the planned responses are implemented. The difference between the pre- and post-response assessments can thus be interpreted as reflecting the expected value of the planned responses.

Projects that use this extension to the techniques of probability and impact assessment do so in order to improve their understanding of the value that is being added by the risk management process and to quantify the assessed risk improvement potential (see p. 100). When managing contingencies, projects may opt to be guided by the evaluation of overall risk calculated on a post-response basis. This would have the advantage of increasing the project's competitiveness. However, this strategy may prove to be too aggressive unless the risk management process has a high level of maturity. Furthermore, if using this approach, the project must ensure that the implications of risk responses are included in the planning process. This makes the risk management and planning processes more complicated, so the project must decide whether or not the overhead involved is worth bearing.

Decision trees

A decision tree is a quantitative method of modelling a project showing the possible effects of each project decision given the prevailing project status and associated risks. Each outcome is assigned a probability of occurrence allowing the most probable outcome to be determined. Alternative actions can be explored in order to identify the most beneficial outcome.

Sensitivity analysis

Sensitivity analysis seeks to examine the sensitivity of a model to individual parameters, risks or options for the project solution. This can be done deterministically by changing one parameter to reflect the estimated boundaries of uncertainty (for example, by changing the productivity rate to ±10 per cent or ±30 per cent). In this way the sensitivity of the outcome is calculated as a function of the modelled variable.

Sensitivity analysis may also be applied to quantitative risk models, including those based on Monte Carlo analysis, decision trees and influence diagrams. A fuller explanation of how sensitivity analysis can be used in combination with Monte Carlo techniques to compare the risk efficiency of project solutions is included in the Appendix and also illustrated in Figure 4.3 (p. 37).

Knowledge-based risk assessment

There are a number of risk assessment models that use a knowledge base formed from data arising from previous projects. These models interrogate the knowledge base using a set of generic questions or variables related to the nature of the project and its environment. A key advantage is that assessments can be made during the earliest phases of a project, during which there may be insufficient information to use more conventional techniques. Used in this way, such risk models can also be used as an early aid to risk identification, since the generic questions or variables can be likened to prompt lists or checklists.

However, although the assessments themselves can be performed quickly, the compilation of a knowledge base requires considerable time and commitment. In addition, a knowledge base acquired within one industry or company is never wholly applicable to another. Knowledge-based risk assessment systems have therefore not yet become widely available.

RISK RESPONSE TECHNIQUES

Risk response is the process of translating risk assessment information into actions. The processes of risk identification and assessment provide data that improve the predictability of project outcome and identify key areas for management attention. However, unless such data are acted upon, much of the opportunity to add value through risk management will be lost. In the risk management process, risk control is delivered through the Plan Responses and Implement phases (see Chapter 4).

Risk management decisions are almost always characterised by choice, even if one of the options is to do nothing. But to exercise the widest choice, it is first necessary to recognise the range of options that are available. A common weakness with project risk management processes in practice is that the action taken is the first reasonable idea that occurs to the person responsible. The risk control techniques described in this section are strategies aimed at prompting an open-minded approach.

Risks may have either adverse or beneficial consequences for the objectives of the project. Risks with an adverse consequence are referred to as threats, and risks that involve a potentially beneficial consequence are referred to as opportunities. Whilst similarities can be drawn between the risk control techniques used for threats and opportunities, there is a difference between the two in terms of the language used to describe actions that can be taken in response to them.

In the case of threats, responses should be implemented that reduce the effect of the threats to the extent that the consequences of response actions do not exceed the likely value of risk reduction. In the case of opportunities, the project should aim to improve one or more of the project objectives in such a way that the cost and implications of the response actions do not exceed the likely value of improvement. The aim of risk control should be to produce a risk-efficient overall project solution.

A risk-efficient solution will not eliminate all threats or realise all opportunities, so plans must be made to manage the outcome of any residual risk.

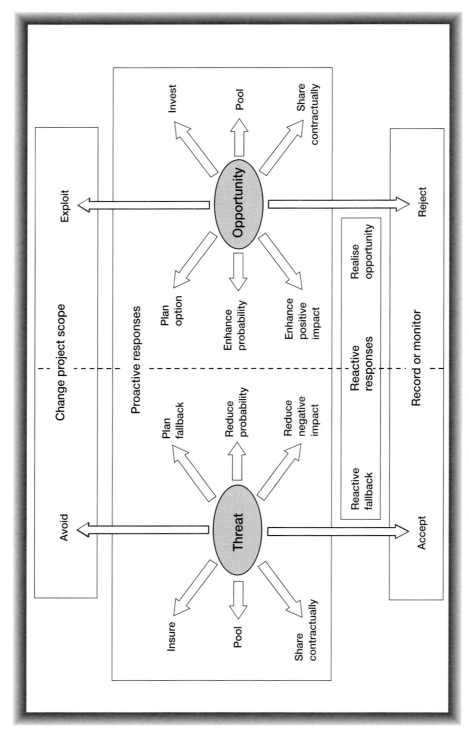

Figure 8.1 *Mirror-imaged summary of risk response strategies*

For threats, a fallback plan will be carried out to minimise the negative impact and, for opportunities, an exploitation plan will be carried out to maximise the positive impact if the opportunity should occur.

Figure 8.1 is a mirror-imaged summary of the approaches that can be used for risk response.

Threat avoidance

Some threats can be avoided by changing objectives or practices so that the cause of the risk can be discounted. For example, a technical threat might be avoided by changing the specification for one of the project's products or a subcontract threat might be avoided by removing a high-risk company from the tendering process. The utility of threat avoidance is limited by its impact on the project objectives – for example, the consequences of avoiding some threats could be unacceptable to stakeholders. Threat avoidance may also reduce the overall risk efficiency of a project solution, so it should be formally reviewed.

The limitations of threat avoidance reflect the fact that risk is inherent to all projects. Indeed, if a project was truly free of risk, it could be fairly criticised as being too cautious or uncompetitive.

Opportunity exploitation

Exploiting an opportunity involves changing the project scope in order to achieve a beneficial outcome for one or more of the stakeholders. If all stakeholders are likely to benefit, this would be a 'win–win' decision, and opposition to such change might be correspondingly low. However, it may be possible to exploit certain opportunities that benefit only one of the stakeholders. Situations like this tend to occur when one aspect of risk exposure has been completely transferred. For example, if a customer has placed a fixed-price contract, it will have transferred all its cost risk to its contractor. If the contractor is able to exploit an opportunity to reduce cost without impacting on the risk retained by the customer (for example, time and product quality), then it would be reasonable for the contractor to exploit the opportunity unilaterally.

An opportunity option is a planned extension to the project scope that would be of benefit should the circumstances of the project evolve in a certain way. As with fallbacks of the kind that change the project solution, options should be formally reviewed at planned points. Project approval often marks the point at which stakeholders become more reluctant to accept changes to scope. For this reason, opportunities are more likely to be exploited successfully before this point. The pre-approval period is therefore often characterised by a drive to maximise the exploitation of opportunities. As a consequence, after project approval the effect of threats on project risk usually outweighs the potential for opportunities.

Reduction of threat probability

Responses that reduce the probability of a threat's occurrence usually require that the risk be tackled at source. Such actions are therefore preventive rather than palliative, and they can be an effective option for risk control. However, the implementation of preventive action usually requires an investment of cost and management time, and this should be justified by costs versus benefits considerations – that is, the cost of implementing the action should be less than the reduction in the risk's expected value.

Enhancement of opportunity probability

Enhancing the probability that an opportunity can eventually be exploited requires a proactive response; such a response might be either strategic or tactical. An example of a strategic response would be a decision to develop a design in-house, rather than to subcontract it, in order to retain greater control over future enhancements. Tactical responses involve the identification of improved methods for project delivery. For example, it may be possible to optimise human resource allocation on a project to increase the probability of reduced cost, or to increase parallel development to increase the probability of an earlier finish to the project stage.

Reduction of the negative impact of threats

Responses that reduce the impact of threats may be either proactive or reactive. The nature of proactive responses is usually concerned with preserving flexibility in the project solution, thus making the project more robust in its ability to absorb adverse events. Flexibility might be maintained by preserving margins within the product design or creating programme flexibility through contracting options or activity sequencing and the like. Proactive control actions are carried out before the threat occurs.

Reactive responses are designed to limit the consequences when the risk occurs. In such cases the response time is key to the effectiveness of risk impact reduction. It is therefore important to define a trigger upon which these reactive responses will be invoked.

Reactive risk reduction responses include increased management attention, the diversion of resources and the prevention of risk impact spreading to other consequences. However, it should be noted that there may be conflicts between these approaches. For example, if resources are diverted to reduce the impact of a certain risk, this is likely to have secondary adverse consequences. In general, proactive approaches produce a more effective control over risk than an exclusive reliance on reactive approaches, which is why it is important for the project's risk assessment processes to be designed to understand the nature of risk at source.

Enhancement of the positive impact of opportunities

Responses that increase the positive impact of opportunities may be proactive or reactive, in the same way as threat reductions. Proactive enhancement may include arranging recognition or payment for early delivery, planning for possible availability of a deliverable earlier than expected, planning for the use of resources available earlier than expected and exploiting the publicity potential of positive impact (for example, advertising early delivery, completion under budget and so on). Reactive enhancement includes implementing any plans or provisions made in advance or redeploying resources as they become available. In general, as for the reduction of negative impact of threats, proactive approaches produce a more effective control over risk than reactive ones, whether planned or unplanned.

Responses that affect both risk probability and impact

The distinction between the effects of responses on probability and impact is a useful prompt. It also provides a logical means of relating the selection of actions to risk assessment information concerned with the source of risks. However, many risk reduction and opportunity enhancement actions tackle both probability and impact. Examples include taking steps to ensure the retention of key resources, implementation of realistic incentives and improvement of the frequency and quality of communication.

Fallbacks

A fallback is a plan of action that would be implemented either if a risk event occurs or if the level of a risk becomes sufficiently unacceptable for an alternative solution to be preferred. A fallback of the former kind is a reactive response designed to minimise risk impact, as described under 'Reduction of the negative impact of threats' above. This kind of fallback may be associated with trigger dates or trigger events that are recorded in order to ensure that the action is implemented in a timely manner.

The second kind of fallback would, if implemented, change the project scope by changing the project solution so as to avoid a threat. Activating the fallback plan would therefore require a decision. This kind of fallback may therefore be associated with a fallback decision point – a date or event on which a decision should be either made or formally deferred. This kind of fallback tends to be more prevalent in the early phases of projects, when there are fewer constraints on the project solution. Experience has shown that the use of fallback decision points can be a very useful tool during such phases.

Opportunity realisation

The realisation of opportunities ensures that potential improvements to the project objectives are delivered. For instance, if there is an opportunity to complete a project task early and release resources, the realisation of that opportunity would be to begin another task early or deliver that task at reduced cost, depending on the priorities of the project objectives.

Risk transfer and share

Risk transfer involves passing on the responsibility for bearing the impact of a threat to another party. Risk transfer may result in an overall reduction to the level of project risk if the party to whom risk is transferred is more capable of managing it. For example, a subcontractor may be used because of its expertise or resources. In some cases, the project strategy may be fundamentally driven by decisions concerning risk ownership. For example Private Finance Initiatives (PFIs) are based on the principle that, by buying a service, a government organisation can transfer the risks associated with delivering the associated infrastructure to the private sector.

However, it is usually not possible, or even desirable, to transfer risk completely, so risk transfer requires a balanced approach that leaves residual risk on both sides. Methods that can be employed for achieving this balance are generally contractual and include liquidated damages, risk-sharing joint ventures, warranties, performance bonds and long-term support.

Some contracting strategies require particularly careful attention to risk ownership and sharing. For example the target cost/incentive fee (TCIF) approach is designed to motivate stakeholders from the perspective of both threats and opportunities. For this to work effectively the target price must be based on a realistic expected project cost. Private/government partnerships should also be founded on a clear understanding of which party should own or share risks of different types. When risk is transferred or shared, the guiding principle should be that responsibility for bearing the consequences of risk should fall on the party that is best able to influence the risk outcome.

Insurance and other financial products

Insurance is a specialised form of threat transfer that is appropriate to providing financial cover for events that are outside the project's control. Typically, the threats covered will have a low probability, but high impact. Insurance plays an important role in financial planning, by allowing contingencies to be operated at a level that does not have to include provision for disaster.

Financial products based on derivatives may be used to play a similar role to insurance. These may be used to provide guaranteed boundaries for exchange rates or material prices.

Pooling risk

A company or organisation may opt to self-insure for certain threats rather than purchase financial protection. The viability of this strategy will depend on factors such as the size of the organisation, the number of projects that it supports and the type of risks involved. If this approach is adopted, projects may participate in a risk pool with other projects. The exposure of each project to risk events that are covered by the risk pool would be calculated at a project level, but the financial cover would be held centrally across the portfolio of projects.

Investment aimed at achieving benefits external to the project

In cases where the project's purpose includes the development of opportunities that are of wider benefit, one or more of the stakeholders may wish to invest in the project by accepting lower levels of profit or contingency in order to fund the exploitation and realisation of opportunities. This would be a rational explanation for the project having taken on an exceptional degree of risk and should be recorded in the project business case. The stakeholders concerned would be responsible for taking this into account when managing the overall risk associated with their project portfolio.

Risk acceptance

Where there is no acceptable or economically viable approach to threat avoidance or reduction, residual risk has to be absorbed and its consequences managed. Time impact may be managed by planning strategies that prevent high-risk activities from being close to the critical path, although this is often not possible. Provision for cost impact should be planned within the budget for financial contingencies. The project should also consider the impact that acceptance of threats will have on its stakeholders and advise them accordingly. Failure to disclose the nature and extent of project threat can lead to loss of trust, which can have long-term adverse commercial consequences.

RISK MANAGEMENT AUDIT TECHNIQUES

Typically risk management audits take one of the following forms:

- verification that a risk management process is being applied as planned
- a capability audit to assess the effectiveness of the risk management process
- a due diligence audit to evaluate the exposure of stakeholders to overall project risk.

This section summarises each type of audit in turn and briefly describes the skills, tools and techniques required.

Risk management verification audit

The most basic type of audit is that which verifies whether or not the risk management process is being applied as planned. The baseline for assessment is the risk management plan, and the data collection techniques could include interviews with project personnel, inspection of risk reports and monitoring trends shown by metrics (such as the frequency with which risks are reviewed). This type of audit may be performed by anyone who is familiar with the risk management plan, but the conclusions are more likely to be accepted if the auditor has a degree of independence from the project.

Risk management capability audit

A capability audit should check not only that the risk management process is being applied as planned, but that it is also based on best practice tailored to the needs of the project. Audit data might be collected in a similar manner to the audit data collected for a more basic type of audit as described above. However, this type of audit requires specialist risk management expertise, since the focus of interest should be on how the effectiveness of the risk management process itself can be improved. The tools used to identify such improvements might include reference to best practice guidance (such as the *PRAM Guide*) and/or a risk maturity model.

A project team may wish to conduct its own internal review of capability, without independent assistance. Self-assessment or team workshops would provide a suitable approach to this activity. Provided that a constructive atmosphere is maintained, this will also help to improve the team's risk management culture. However, it would be incorrect to label such an activity as an audit. The term risk management process 'healthcheck' is more appropriate.

Risk management due diligence audit

Due diligence audits are usually sponsored by stakeholders at critical decision points, in order to provide assurance that the project's exposure to risk is within acceptable limits. This type of audit should include an assessment of the capability of the risk management process itself, but should also be extended to examine the integrity of all the related processes and data. In particular, it should include a critical examination of the major risks, and consider any influences that motivation or conflicts of interest might have on estimating bias. The due diligence auditor must be able to combine specialist risk management skills with experience in the type of project concerned. They must also have sufficient independence from the project for stakeholders to have confidence in the conclusions and recommendations.

Risk maturity models

A risk maturity model provides a structured approach to assessing the capability of a risk management process. A number of models have been developed, most of which recognise four discrete levels of risk management maturity. The deployment of some of these models has now been sufficient to show that they can help organisations to:

- benchmark the risk management capability of their projects
- identify prioritised actions and achievable targets for process improvement
- identify areas of weakness or strength that are common to the organisation's projects
- identify projects that have points of excellence for other projects to learn from.

The four levels adopted by most risk maturity models can be compared to the five levels defined by the Software Engineering Institute (SEI) capability maturity model, from which most maturity models claim some degree of ancestry. The absence of a fifth level for risk maturity models is generally justified by the difficulties that might be faced by an organisation that tried to achieve perfection in every individual aspect of its risk management process. Achieving the peak of excellence in several aspects of a risk management process simultaneously might lead to some benefits being cancelled out. For example, a risk management process that requires the maintenance of a great deal of information might prove to be insufficiently flexible to facilitate rapid risk responses. In practice, risk management is but one of a number of project management processes and should only be carried out to the extent that it adds value.

RISK MANAGEMENT TOOLS

Having selected a combination of risk management techniques, a project should turn its attention to the tools that it will use to undertake the processes involved. This section describes the various types of risk management tool that are in common use. In each case there are a number of commercial products available on the market. However, it is not the policy of the *PRAM Guide* to recommend any particular product. Instead, the notes are provided against each type of tool to indicate their functionality and help users discriminate between different products.

Risk databases (single PC applications)

The purpose of a risk management database tool is to maintain and report on the records arising from risk identification, assessment and control. These contents are often referred to as the risk register. As a minimum, the database should include all the risk register fields noted in the Appendix.

It is possible for projects to develop their own database tools. The simplest approach is to develop a template using a spreadsheet or word processor. However, the cost of professional stand-alone risk database tools is relatively low, and in most cases they are likely to provide better value for money.

A professional tool should allow the user to define the criteria used by each project to define the probability and impact criteria. In addition, reporting should be supported by a flexible approach to sorting and filtering data. Further to this, projects should consider the ways in which the database supports the following five points. These have been listed in their likely ranking of importance.

1 **Communication**. A database maintains records, but its most important practical function is to facilitate communication on risk issues. Indeed, without the presence of good communication, the risk data itself is likely to be of poor quality. Accordingly, the project should take care to understand who will require risk information, what information they need and how it is best presented.

2 **Action tracking**. The implementation of responses to control risk is likely to be the primary purpose of the risk management process. It follows that the database and reporting mechanisms should facilitate the way in which responses are selected, allocated and reviewed.

3 **Financial control**. Where risk data is used for the calculation and control of financial contingencies, the risk database should be capable of handling the relevant data. This could include the potential cost of risk impact, the cost of risk responses, the expected cost of risk impact post-response and information that supports the rationale for such data.

4 **Integration with quantitative risk management**. A risk management database is primarily a tool for the management of qualitative risk data. However, if techniques such as Monte Carlo analysis are also used by the project, then much of the underlying data for quantitative analysis should be present in the risk database. Similarly, it may be appropriate to use results emerging from quantitative analysis for reporting and prioritisation sorting purposes.

5 **Electronic compatibility**. Software compatibility with other reporting tools may be an important issue. The most common requirement is for ease of importing into word-processed documents. This may in itself be an important aspect of the use of risk reports for communication.

Use of a stand-alone PC database is likely to suit the purposes of smaller projects. The main drawback is the lack of concurrent write access. This is no problem if data entry and report generation is restricted to a single individual, but it becomes increasingly inefficient if several users are involved. Larger projects and project-based organisations may find that a specialist networked risk database tool is required.

Risk databases (Internet/intranet tools)

Risk database tools that make use of either the Internet or an intranet allow risk data to be viewed and/or changed concurrently by a number of users. This can be a very significant advantage for communication, particularly within large organisations, or in circumstances where the users are geographically dispersed.

For many large organisations an important tool selection factor is the integration of project and business risk management processes. Guidance for companies listed on the London Stock Exchange, issued by the Turnbull

Committee in 1999, makes a number of recommendations in respect of the ways in which they should oversee the management of risk. For project-based companies this has created the requirement for a process that assimilates, rationalises and promulgates risk data to all levels within the company. Some Internet risk tools are able to assist in this process by allowing users access to a common risk database, and giving them views of the data that are tailored to the scope and level of their responsibility.

A significant drawback to the use of networked risk tools is that of cost. The purchase cost of such tools is many times greater than that for an equivalent product designed to run on a stand-alone PC. Added to this, there are training, maintenance and IT infrastructure costs. Rolling out a new network-based risk management tool is therefore a major undertaking.

Another factor that should not be underestimated is the effort required to gain sufficient buy-in from all personnel who will be expected to use the tool. Ideally, everyone on the project who has direct involvement with the risk management process should regularly use the tool to record, maintain and review risk data that is relevant to their work. Project personnel who are actively engaged with the risk management process in this way are much more likely to be committed to maintaining realistic assessments and implementing risk responses. Giving write access to project personnel also reduces the time spent by the risk analyst on data entry. However, experience shows that it takes a lot of time, training and commitment to achieve this level of participation. At a minimum, the risk analyst would still need to provide regular guidance on the quantification of risks, since experience shows that this is an area in which the idiosyncratic approaches taken by individuals produce very inconsistent data.

Despite these drawbacks, the act of installing access to risk data on every relevant person's computer can have a very beneficial effect on a project's risk management culture. For a very large project or project-based organisation, the variance produced by risk is likely to have substantial cost implications, so the cost associated with providing an effective risk management tool may be small in comparison. Thus, provided that factors that are concerned with utility and ease of use are addressed, a networked risk database tool has the potential to add economic value.

As a guide, the following lists of features and functions is provided to indicate the selection criteria that might be used when procuring an Internet-enabled risk database tool. They have been listed in an order of priority that is consistent with the importance that usability has to the achievement of added value.

Technical features

1   Compatibility with the project's IT environment, including security constraints
2   Robustness/reliability of software
3   Ease of use and speed, including conditions under which the tool is being heavily used – ability to locate, sort and filter quickly; ease of data entry

4   Clarity of the user interface – ability to see associated relevant data on one screen
5   Minimisation of bespoke features
6   Control of access rights for read and write
7   Flexibility provided by project-definable fields (used for classification, sorting and filtering of risks)
8   Clarity of reports/ease with which bespoke reports can be created and maintained
9   Commonality of tool with potential customers (for example, to form a joint risk register, or to facilitate reporting)
10 Ability to export data to other tools for further analysis or reports (usually involving export into Excel or Word)
11 Ability to export information and reports for electronic distribution
12 Automated recording processes for history
13 Concurrent access from geographically dispersed sites

Risk functionality

1   Effectiveness of the risk response functions as an action items database
2   Ability to rank risks for reports (using the P-I matrix approach and others)
3   Facilitation of the management of both opportunity-and threat-based risks
4   Project-definable criteria for probability and impact (up to five by five classification); automated classification of probability and time and cost impacts as high, medium and so on, dependent on the values of the values entered and project definable criteria
5   Flexible filtering to focus on groups of risks or mitigation actions; ability to combine filtering with risk ranking
6   Ability to relate risks to project defined hierarchies including work, organisation and cost breakdown structures (WBS, OBS and CBS)
7   Traffic lights function to indicate risk severity, aligned with user definable 'pain/gain thresholds'
8   Interested parties fields and facilities for enhancing communication
9   Process for the control of approval status for new and ongoing risks
10 Maintenance of data used for quantitative risk analysis, including correlation data and three-point estimates for cost and schedule impact
11 Facilitation of the management of issues
12 Ability to interface with other project management tools as desired
13 Ease of integration with the selected quantitative risk analysis tool

Monte Carlo analysis tools

The techniques used for Monte Carlo analysis are explained in greater detail in Appendix A3.3. At the most basic levels, the process requires that an outcome for each activity (for example, cost or duration) in the risk model be assigned a probability distribution function. Typically, this is defined using a three-point estimate. However, realistic simulation will normally require that some or all of the following features are included in the risk model:

- differentiation between the variable outcomes of planned activities and risks for which there is a probability of occurrence associated with a variable 'step change'
- statistical dependencies to simulate correlation between activity outcomes
- use of different probability distributions within the same model
- stochastic (probabilistic) branching.

Experience shows that that failure to use these features as and when appropriate produces analysis results that understate the realistic levels of overall project risk. Some of the reasons for this are explained in Appendix A3.3. The project should therefore take time to understand why and how it will use Monte Carlo analysis, and how this might affect its selection of the tool.

Most tools designed for Monte Carlo analysis fall into one of four categories:

1 specialist risk analysis tools that can be used to run Monte Carlo simulation
2 tools that are able to extract data from common planning tools and put them into a format that is suitable for analysis using a specialist Monte Carlo analysis tool
3 risk database tools that include a Monte Carlo analysis package
4 planning tools that include a Monte Carlo risk management function.

Specialist risk analysis tools tend to have a superior functionality as compared to planning or database tools that include a risk analysis function. Some are also much better suited to the production of graphical reports. This has created a demand for tools that are able to extract data from planning tools or databases and put it into a format (such as a spreadsheet) that can be handled by a specialist Monte Carlo tool. Tools of the type listed as (1) and (2) above are therefore often used in combination.

However, there is a wide range in the capability and utility of Monte Carlo functions offered by different planning and database tools of the types listed as (3) and (4) above. The tools that a project has selected for its project planning and risk database management might therefore already have all the Monte Carlo functionality required. In this case there would be no good reason for buying an additional specialist Monte Carlo risk analysis tool.

Despite this, the advice of this *Guide* is that the project should choose its tools for planning and risk database management primarily on the basis of their suitability for the processes that they serve. The presence of an integrated Monte Carlo analysis function is usually only a secondary advantage, and some integrated tools may not have sufficient functionality to produce a realistic evaluation of overall project risk.

APPLICABILITY OF RISK TECHNIQUES

This chapter has described some of the most common techniques for the identification, assessment and control of project risks. The techniques for risk control are potentially applicable at any stage in any project. However, a project will normally only select a subset of the identification and assessment techniques described. This selection should depend on the considerations listed at the start of this chapter and should also take into account factors such as project size and the requirements of its stakeholders. In addition, the project should adopt an audit strategy that provides assurance that the process is effective. Accordingly, this chapter concludes with a summary of the applicability of each identification, assessment and audit technique. This summary is shown in the Tables 8.1 to 8.3 below.

Table 8.1 Risk identification techniques

Technique	Also used for:		Applicability		Resources	
	Risk assessment	Risk control	Pre-project approval	Post-project approval	Time and/ or cost	Expertise required
Assumptions analysis	P	L	G	G	L	L
Constraints analysis	P	L	G	L	L	L
Checklists	N	N	P	G	M	L
Prompt lists	N	N	G	G	L	L
Brainstorming	L	N	G	G	L	M
Interviews	G	P	P	G	M	M
SWOT analysis	L	P	P	L	L	M
Stakeholder analysis	P	L	G	L	M	M
Project monitoring	P	G	N	G	L	L
Nominal group technique	L	N	G	L	L	M
Delphi technique	L	N	P	L	M	H
Technology readiness levels	P	L	P	L	H	H
Peer review	L	N	G	L	L	H
Reporting by team members	L	L	L	G	L	L

G = Good – strong application.
P = Potential application.
L = Limited application.
N = Not applicable.

H = High resource requirement.
M = Medium resource requirement.
L = Low resource requirement.

Table 8.2 Risk assessment techniques

Technique	Also used for:		Applicability		Resources	
	Risk identification	Risk control	Pre-project approval	Post-project approval	Time and/or cost	Expertise required
Probability assessment	N	N	G	G	L	L
Impact assessment	N	N	G	G	L	L
Descriptions meta-language	P	P	P	G	L	M
Influence diagrams	P	P	G	L	M	M
Risk breakdown structures	G	L	G	P	M	H
Probability-impact matrix	N	N	P	G	L	L
Risk improvement potential	N	N	G	P	M	M
Risk impact windows	N	P	N	P	M	M
Expected value	N	N	P	G	L	M
Risk register	N	G	P	G	M	L
Roll-up indicators	N	L	L	G	H	L
Probability distributions	L	N	G	P	M	H
Three-point estimates	P	N	G	P	M	H
First-pass quantitative model	P	L	G	L	L	M
Monte Carlo analysis	P	L	G	P	M	H
Correlation	L	N	G	P	L	H
Post-response analysis	N	P	P	G	M	H
Decision trees	N	G	P	L	M	H
Sensitivity analysis	P	P	P	L	M	M
Knowledge-based models	G	L	G	N	H	H

G = Good – strong application.   H = High resource requirement.
P = Potential application.   M = Medium resource requirement.
L = Limited application.   L = Low resource requirement.
N = Not applicable.

Table 8.3 Risk audit techniques

Technique	Also includes:			Applicability		Resources	
	Risk identification	Risk assessment	Risk control	Pre-project approval	Post-project approval	Time and/ or cost	Expertise required
Verification audit	N	N	N	P	G	L	M
Capability audit	L	L	P	G	G	M	H
Due diligence	P	P	G	G	L	H	H

G = Good – strong application.   H = High resource requirement.
P = Potential application.   M = Medium resource requirement.
L = Limited application.   L = Low resource requirement.
N = Not applicable.

Appendix:
Using Risk Management Techniques

This appendix describes some of the techniques available to the risk practitioner. It builds on the descriptions given in Chapter 8 and suggests ways in which the techniques might be applied. This appendix can only give limited details, and the practitioner should refer to more detailed handbooks or textbooks where necessary.

A1 IDENTIFICATION TECHNIQUES

A1.1 Assumptions and constraints analysis

Assumptions and constraints analysis allows some of the key risks to be identified and is most easily applied if a project has formally recorded all assumptions made as part of the bid or project definition process. Assumptions are statements of belief concerning future events and they underpin the project definition. Threats could emerge if such assumptions were proven to be incorrect. Constraints are limitations that are assumed to apply to the project's objectives and plans. Opportunities could emerge if such constraints are modified.

The analysis involves three steps:

1   Identify assumptions and constraints.
2   Assess assumptions and constraints.
3   Allocate ownership of identified risks and forward for formal risk assessment.

A1.1.1 Identify assumptions and constraints

During the initial stages of the project, as a detailed understanding of the objectives is built up and the plans to deliver the objectives evolve, it is always necessary to make assumptions. Project constraints will also become identifiable. For complex projects, an assumptions database or register may be required, which can also assist in assumptions management and provide traceability on how assumptions have been handled. The comprehensive identification of assumptions and constraints can be assisted by including a formal review in the project initiation start-up phase, for the specific purpose of identifying and recording all assumptions made to date. This review could be structured so that it systematically addresses the overall project objectives and all work areas – for example, by making reference to the work breakdown structure (WBS).

One advantage of assumptions and constraints analysis is that it can cover a wide range of issues, thus giving breadth to the risk identification process. To achieve this, it is important to record assumptions that are implicit to the project definition as well as those that are explicitly stated in work packages and so on. Typically, the following areas might be included:

- project purposes and the prioritisation of objectives
- ownership of the project stakeholders and their financial/operational viability
- capability of suppliers and their willingness to disclose the truth
- commercial assumptions, including contracting strategies
- resource assumptions (availability and capability of human and physical resources)
- validity of estimating processes and metrics
- effectiveness of the project's organisation and its management processes
- outcome of ongoing technological changes
- assumptions concerning standards and legal requirements, and their implications
- financial assumptions such as inflation, exchange rates and cost of borrowing
- the objectives of other projects and their timings.

It is important to ensure that a mechanism exists for identifying and recording assumptions and constraints wherever they are made throughout the project. The project team should be educated to be aware of assumptions and be encouraged (or required) to test their areas of responsibility regularly in order to identify any aspect where they are assuming something that is uncertain. Assumptions can be made at any stage of the project life cycle and at any level of the project team. The project's exposure to them may also change as time goes on. Assumptions and constraints analysis should therefore be undertaken on a regular basis if all potential risks are to be identified.

A1.1.2 *Assess assumptions and constraints*

Each assumption and constraint can be tested using two standard questions which, together, will indicate whether or not a risk can be identified. The two questions cover the stability of the assumption or constraint and the sensitivity of the project to it. They can be framed as follows:

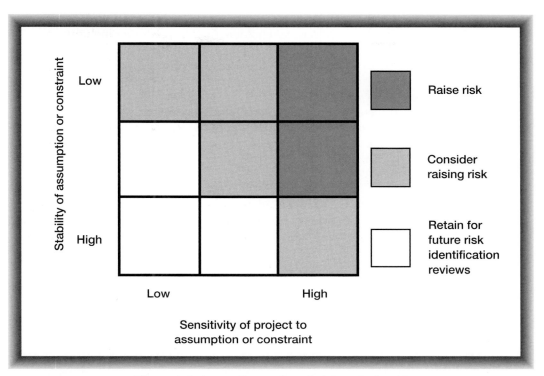

Figure A.1 *Assumptions and constraints analysis grid*

- **Stability.** How likely is the assumption or constraint to be proved correct? High/medium/low scales may be used for this, or a more direct assessment of likelihood can be made using a percentage probability estimate.
- **Sensitivity.** How important is the assumption or constraint in terms of its influence over the project objectives? Quantitative information might be available from a sensitivity analysis. Alternatively, the question might be addressed qualitatively using categories such as crucial (high importance), significant (medium importance) and minor (low importance).

Having assessed each assumption and constraint in these two dimensions, they can be placed on a grid similar to that shown in Figure A.1. Items that are crucial to the project objectives and have a significant likelihood of occurrence should be identified as risks. Consideration should also be given to identifying other items as risks if they could be of sufficient significance to warrant specific management.

A1.1.3 Allocate ownership of identified risks and forward for formal risk assessment

This is the last stage in all risk identification processes. The project should have a policy on ownership of risks in two senses, namely:

- a process for agreeing the risk-owning organisation, based on the boundaries of responsibility between stakeholders (including those risks that are shared)
- the criteria used to select the individual responsible for managing each risk.

Having identified the appropriate ownership at these levels, the risk should be promptly passed forward for the attention of the person who is responsible for the formal risk assessment.

A1.2 Checklists

Checklists offer a powerful means of identifying risks from learned experience. They also permit rapid risk identification, allowing the busy project manager to generate a list of potential risks quickly.

A1.2.1 Sources of checklists

An organisation may wish to use a standard checklist developed for their particular industry. Several checklists are available, such as those pertaining to defence procurement, software engineering, construction, IT and the offshore industry.

However, it is often preferable for each organisation to develop its own specific checklist. This can be done by capturing information concerning risk events as they occur on projects. The aim should be to produce a list that can be used by project managers of future projects to ensure that they consider whether such risks could be applicable to their own projects. Any risk that has occurred should be considered for inclusion in the checklist, although risks that have only occurred on one project or only had a minor impact might be omitted.

The production of an organisation-specific checklist is only possible if there is a process for monitoring and recording risks that have actually occurred. As a minimum, this might be achieved as part of a formal post-project review conducted at the end of each project.

A1.2.2 Producing an organisation-specific checklist

Where an organisation produces its own specific list, ownership of the master list must be clearly defined. An in-house risk specialist may be given the responsibility of developing and maintaining the checklist, but not every organisation is in a position to use an in-house specialist.

Since the purpose of a checklist is to ensure that lessons are learned from past experience, it must be kept up-to-date. The checklist content should therefore be regularly reconciled against the outcome of recent projects. In doing this, care should be taken that the content of the additional questions is sufficiently generic to detect the presence of equivalent circumstances on other projects. Over time it is also possible that changes to the nature of the organisation's projects will result in some checklist questions becoming redundant. A checklist's utility may start to decline if it exceeds 100 questions.

A1.2.3 Checklist structure

A checklist is usually written as a series of questions arranged in groups. These groups can be arranged using a source-oriented hierarchy (risk breakdown structure) to ensure that the list has sufficient breadth. Table A.1. shows an example of a two-level hierarchical structure for part of a checklist. A third level could be introduced to provide a more detailed list of questions, each one of which has a sharper focus. For example, a ship construction company could break up the question related to key skills into a list of specific skills and trades. The disadvantages of maintaining a third level would include growth in the number of questions and the possibility that questions might become too focused for the detection of wider risks. In practice, an organisation might therefore choose to develop only certain branches of its second-level questions into greater detail, or not to develop a third level at all.

Since the checklist is based upon learned experience, it is useful to maintain a record of traceability to previous projects. The three right-hand columns in Table A.1. illustrate one way of doing this.

Records of the extent to which risk has impacted on previous projects can be useful from a number of perspectives. By knowing which projects experienced a high-risk impact in equivalent circumstances, a project manager should be able to contact the people involved to obtain more detailed advice. Equally, valuable advice might be gained from projects that experienced a 'nil' impact of risk, since they might have used effective approaches to risk avoidance.

A1.2.4 Using the checklist

Answers of 'Yes' or 'Not applicable' to the checklist questions shown in Table A.1. would suggest that the project was not exposed to significant risk from the associated source. In contrast, consideration should be given to raising risks in the case of each question for which the answer is 'No' or 'Uncertain'.

Any question to which the answer is 'Uncertain' should be classified as a risk provided that the potential consequences are sufficiently significant.

A 'No' answer indicates the presence of a problem, which may be identified as being a risk, depending on the circumstances of the project and the extent to which associated factors may cause variance to the project outcome. However, in some cases, 'No' answers will simply identify issues that must be addressed by the normal project planning process or difficulties for which the implications are well understood. An advantage of the checklist process is that it can be used to identify issues and opportunities, as well as risk threats.

Table A.1 Example of a checklist based on a two-level risk breakdown structure

				Previous impacts		
Risk type	Risk source	Question	N/A yes, no, or uncertain	Project A	Project B	Project C
Requirement	Completeness	Have all requirements been identified and quantified		Nil	High	Low
	Clarity	Are the requirements well understood and free of significant ambiguities?		Low	High	Low
	Difficulty	Is it possible to achieve all requirements without any particular technical difficulty?		Med	Low	Low
	Flexibility	Is there sufficient flexibility to absorb impact of failures to achieve difficult requirements?		Med	High	Med
	Stability	Are there unlikely to be significant changes to the requirements?		Nil	High	Nil
	Complexity	Are the requirements sufficiently simple to be well understood, estimated and planned?		Nil	Low	Med
	Proof of design	Will it be straightforward to prove compliance with the design requirements?		Low	Med	Low
Human Resources	Manpower	Has the organisation got sufficient manpower to resource this project?		Med	Nil	Nil
	Key people	Can the project continue to operate smoothly if any individual leaves?		High	Nil	Nil
	Key skills	Has the organisation got sufficient people available with the key skills required?		Med	Low	Nil
	Experience	Has the organisation got sufficient people available with the experience required?		Med	Med	Nil
	Location	Will the project be sufficiently well staffed at the required location(s)?		Nil	Nil	Med
…etc. ⇓					⇒	…etc.

A1.3 Prompt lists

Prompt lists are used to help ensure that all aspects of a project are covered when attempting to identify a project's risks. Their purpose is to stimulate lateral thinking and encourage a broad perspective to risk identification. For this reason they can also be used to structure other techniques for risk identification, such as brainstorming.

The most common form of prompt list is one based on generic risk factors or risk breakdown structures associated with the type of business with which the project is concerned. Organisations may wish to recommend prompt lists for use in different circumstances. The following list is a fairly general example.

- Contracting strategy
- Stakeholder interests
- Management effectiveness
- Supplier performance
- Alignment of motives
- Human resources
- Physical resources
- Technological change
- Technical difficulty
- Project/programme complexity
- Knowledge and information
- Financial uncertainties
- Ability to specify
- Contract acceptance
- Schedule adherence
- Estimating processes
- Assumptions
- Constraints
- External events

A prompt list should not be exhaustive, but should simply be used as a focus of attention, or viewpoint, in the identification of risks. There will often be a number of subsections for each category, and these can be expected to produce overlaps. However, whether a risk falls into one category or another should not be of great concern, only that the risk is identified.

It is also possible to identify risks more systematically by treating plans or project breakdown structures in the manner of a prompt list. If combined with lists based on generic risk factors or risk breakdown structures, this will provide an approach that brings both depth and breadth to the risk identification process. Like checklists, prompt lists may also be used to identify issues and opportunities as well as threats.

A1.4 Brainstorming

Brainstorming is used widely as a method of problem-solving and idea evaluation. It has also become widely recognised as a technique for risk identification. However, the classic brainstorming technique needs modification if it
is to be used for risk identification rather than problem-solving, since the
objective is to produce a list of candidate items for risks that can be assessed
in more depth at a later time.

A facilitator and recorder should be appointed to run a risk identification
brainstorming session. Sometimes these roles can be combined. The facilitator should be responsible for the conduct of the meeting and preparing a
suitable structure for it. Ideally, he or she should have a degree of independence from the team, but also a good understanding of the project's objectives
and environment. A totally independent facilitator would therefore need to
be given adequate preparation time.

The recorder should capture risks in a way that is visible to all participants
– for example, using a flipchart or white board. It is often also helpful to
record bullet-pointed supporting data (for example, causes of exposure to
risk, potential trigger factors and associations between risks). The other item
of data that must be captured is the name of the person who, provisionally,
will be responsible for leading the later assessment of each risk. The objective
is to capture sufficient information to launch the risk assessment process.

Typically the rules of a brainstorming session are as follows:

1 Encourage wide participation – prevent the meeting from being domi-
   nated by a minority.
2 Ask for quantity rather than in-depth analysis (sorting the wheat from
   the chaff comes later).
3 Encourage participants to build on the ideas of others – seek combination
   and improvement.
4 Prohibit overt criticism – to encourage participation and defer judgement.

Thought should be given to structuring a brainstorming session so that
risks are identified from a wide perspective. A common fault with many risk
management processes is that risks are only identified from a narrow
perspective, such as technical difficulties or cost impact. To counter this a
brainstorming session can be structured around prompt lists tailored to the
project environment, but designed to cover a wide range of risk sources. This
structure can be supplemented with impact-oriented prompts, such as
project critical success criteria, or other source-oriented prompts, such as
critical success drivers.

An experienced facilitator will have a multi-layered approach to structuring brainstorming sessions. In many cases it may only be necessary to use a
high-level set of prompts and allow participants to use these as points from
which to explore various levels of detail. However, if the meeting needs
more stimulation, a lower-level set of sub-prompts is a useful standby.

Another approach to structuring a brainstorming session is to use a WBS (work breakdown structure) or PBS (product breakdown structure). This ensures that the session covers all project activities and deliverables. The disadvantage of this approach is that its technical orientation can result in some important sources of risk being overlooked. It is important that 'whole project' risks are also identified and included in the session, as these risks are often the most important. The use of a prompt list or risk breakdown structure can help to ensure that all areas are covered.

It is good practice to include a briefing period at the beginning of the brainstorming session. This should include an explanation of the purpose of the meeting and how its output will be used. It may also be useful to remind participants of the baseline from which risk is being identified. As a minimum, this baseline should be summarised as a high-level statement of critical success criteria. Finally, it is often helpful to remind participants of the meaning of the word 'risks' as distinct from, say, 'issues'.

The target time for a brainstorming session is typically three to four hours. A productive timetable might be as follows:

Briefing	(10 minutes)
Explanation of structure(s) to be used	(10 minutes)
Identify risks	(90 minutes)
Review, rationalise risk list and assign owners	(90 minutes)

A1.5 Risk interviews

Many risk identification techniques involve gaining information from groups of people. However, it is often necessary to obtain detailed perspectives that cannot be explored through group dialogue, and interviews provide the ideal means for doing this. Interviews may also provide the means for discussing information that individuals would be reluctant to introduce during group sessions. Interviews can therefore be used for a variety of purposes, including:

- risk identification
- assessing and reviewing identified risks (for example, estimating probabilities and impacts, planning risk responses, identifying fallbacks and secondary risks)
- estimating data to be used for quantitative analysis (for example, probability distributions, three-point estimates, correlation factors).

Effective interviewing is an essential (and often underestimated) skill of the risk practitioner. The effectiveness of risk interviews will depend on the interpersonal skills of the interviewer and the nature of their relationship with the interviewee. There is also a subtle balance to be struck between providing structure (in the interests of effectiveness and efficiency) and freedom for the interviewee to respond with unanticipated, yet relevant, information. The following guidelines are aimed at helping the risk practitioner conduct risk interviews.

1 There is no substitute for thorough preparation. The risk practitioner must ensure that he or she is fully familiar with the project, the interviewee's role in the project and the interviewee's expertise. The interviewee must also prepare adequately by considering any risks in his or her area of responsibility and ensuring that there will be access to any data or information that is likely to be required during the interview.

2 The risk interview must have clear objectives. The objectives should be set by the risk practitioner and communicated clearly to the interviewee both before the interview and at its commencement. To this end, the risk practitioner should have prepared sufficient structure for the aims of the interview to be accomplished in the time allowed. It is very helpful for this structure (or agenda) to be communicated in the invitation to the interview both verbally and in writing.

3 The interview must be conducted in a conducive environment, away from interruptions and distractions, so that the interviewee feels comfortable and relaxed. The interviewee should also be clear as to why the interview is important, how the information will be used and the extent to which it may be attributable: he or she will not contribute freely unless he or she has confidence in the integrity of the process and the purposes for which information will be used.

4 Time management during the interview is important. Interviews should not normally exceed two hours, and most should be much shorter. The interviewer must ensure that momentum is maintained. This is best achieved by using sufficient structure to focus on important aspects of risk. For example, in order to develop a risk description, it is often appropriate to use structured questions such as 'What might make the difference as to whether or not this risk occurs?' and 'If this risk occurs, what factors would influence its outcome?'. The interview should be directed to the extent necessary to focus topics for discussion, but should also be non-directive so that the interviewee is able to explore the subject and express opinions and evaluations. There should also be sufficient flexibility within the interview duration to allow for unplanned diversions to be explored, since these may reveal previously unrecognised risks or perspectives.

5 The interviewer should ask open questions to encourage the interviewee to contribute freely. Closed questions (that is, questions for which there is only a right or wrong answer) should only be used when strictly necessary. Although the interviewer, by virtue of his or her interaction with other team members, may be able to contribute contextual information, he or she must try to avoid leading the interviewee into giving the 'right' answer. Although difficult to achieve, the aim should be to avoid bias being generated in the interviewee's responses.

6   The relationship between the interviewer and interviewee will determine the success or otherwise of the interview. It is therefore important that the interviewer strives to be non-judgemental. The interviewer must be aware of non-verbal clues, such as body language, ensuring that the interviewee remains comfortable and willing to participate in the interview. However, this must be balanced by a willingness to challenge and probe the interviewee to identify assumptions or bias and to validate the information that is being presented.

7   Clear and unambiguous records of the interview must be made. This is best done at the time of the interview, rather than relying on memory after the event. If the notes taken at the time of the interview are in rough form, the interviewee should be given (or have easy access to) a final version of the interview's products at the earliest opportunity. If these products consist of entries in a risk register or database, these entries could be made in the course of the interview, provided that doing so does not interrupt the interview's flow. In such circumstances, giving the interviewee real-time access to the database is likely to increase the value that they attach to it.

Many general management textbooks offer advice and guidelines on inter-personal skills and interviewing techniques. Risk practitioners should use best practice from these sources, while ensuring that the interview meets the specific requirements of the risk process.

A1.6 Stakeholder analysis

Stakeholders are people, groups or organisations with interests in a project or programme. Primary stakeholders are those directly affected, whilst secondary stakeholders are those who may have an indirect influence over a project. Key stakeholders are those who can significantly influence decisions and are strongly aligned for or against the project. At a minimum, these will normally include the project sponsor (or customer) and the organisation (or company) that is responsible for project delivery.

Stakeholder analysis should be undertaken at the start of a project to ensure that the stakeholders and their interests are identified. This information can then be used to develop project assumptions and objectives and to identify some of the key risks. Such risks will be associated with project objectives for which there may be conflicts of interest between stakeholders. Whenever the project, its objectives and risks are reconsidered, a stakeholder analysis will be useful. The reconsideration of objectives is likely to be part of the cyclical risk management process prior to project approval as shown in Figure 4.2 (p. 33). However, annual monitoring reviews and major reviews could also include stakeholder analysis as part of their toolkit.

Stakeholder analysis includes the identification of a project's key stakeholders, a thorough assessment of stakeholder interests and concerns and an understanding of how these issues impact on the project, its viability and its exposure to risks. The process is concerned with not only establishing who the key stakeholders are for a specific project, but also what they know, believe and suspect. From this basis it can be established how much of this is valid information and how much is myth, misinformation or rumour. In order for the analysis to be effective it is therefore essential that a profile be developed of each of the stakeholders and public groups.

In addition to bringing their own perspective to the risk identification process, stakeholders may also introduce fresh ideas that the project team would have otherwise overlooked. By developing project requirements that maximise the project's attractiveness to stakeholders while minimising potential conflicts, the stakeholder analysis process might in itself be deployed as an early risk response strategy.

Stakeholder analysis employs logical frameworks that contribute to the project design and assist the identification and implementation of appropriate forms of stakeholder participation to mitigate project risks. There are four logical steps to completing a stakeholder analysis which, when completed, will result in a project stakeholder matrix as shown in Figure A.2.

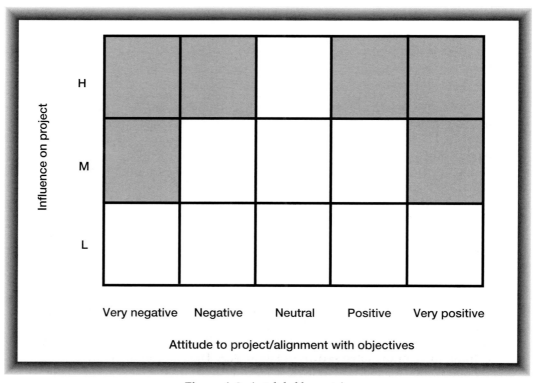

Figure A.2 *A stakeholder matrix*

A1.6.1 Step 1: Stakeholder identification

The project team identifies all the people, organisations, groups and parties that will influence the project or be affected by it. These are recorded in a stakeholder table (see Figure A.3).

Stakeholder name	Stakeholder interests or concerns in the project	Assessment of impact	Potential strategies for reducing the impacts
		L/M/H	

Figure A.3 *A stakeholder table*

A1.6.2 Step 2: Stakeholder interests and concerns

For each stakeholder identified, the team lists the stakeholder's anticipated interests or concerns in the project and considers the impact of the project and any possible changes on the stakeholder. These are detailed in the second column of the table shown in Figure A.3 or compiled in a stakeholder/objectives matrix, an example of which is shown in Figure A.4.

A1.6.2.1 Risk identification

Risks may be identified where certain stakeholders disagree with an objective, or where there are potential conflicts between the objectives of different stakeholders. The severity of each risk will depend on the influence that each stakeholder may have and the extent to which they may be willing to trade off what they perceive to be adverse objectives with other positive aspects of the project.

A1.6.3 Step 3: Assessment of stakeholder impacts

Each stakeholder's impact on the project and on the project risks is assessed, both in terms of their risk to the project or their influence in the management of project risks. An impact of low, medium or high is allocated in column three of the table shown in Figure A.3. The stakeholders can now be plotted on the stakeholder matrix (Figure A.2) according to their influence (L/M/H) and alignment with objectives. Attention will be directed to the

Project objectives	Local authority	Water company	Gas board	Electricity board	Local residents	MPs & councillors
			Stakeholders			etc.
Objective A	✔	○	○	○	✘	✔
Objective B	✔	○	○	○	✘	✔
Objective C	✔	○	○	○	✔	✔
Objective D	✔	✔	✔	✔	○	○
etc.						

Objectives

A – Construct a business park for 20 businesses with full services.

B – Construct highway infrastructure to access the business park.

C – Minimise noise and inconvenience during construction.

D – Robust maintenance regime that provides whole-life value.

Opinion of objectives

✔ Agrees

✘ Disagrees

○ Neutral

Figure A.4 *Part of a stakeholder/objectives matrix for the construction of a business park*

key stakeholders in the shaded areas (high influence and high negative or positive alignment). However, the possibility of combinations of stakeholders should also be considered. For instance, a stakeholder with high negative alignment but low influence might combine with a neutral high-influence stakeholder (for example, media or local councillor) to produce an influential stakeholder group with a highly negative alignment.

A1.6.4 Step 4: Potential strategies for reducing stakeholder impacts

The final column of the matrix considers the strategies that should be put in place to reduce the negative impact of the project on the stakeholders, reduce adverse stakeholder effects on the project or identify processes through which the stakeholders can assist the project risk management. Attention should be paid to ways in which neutral stakeholders with high influence can be brought into alignment with the project's objectives (or vice versa).

The most visible benefits of undertaking stakeholder analysis as part of the risk management process include:

● a sound basis for choice
● improvements for external clients as a result of clearly understanding their real requirements and objectives

- an enhanced understanding of the project's aims on the part of everyone involved
- decisions supported by the stakeholders.

A1.7 Nominal group technique

NGT is a variant of the brainstorming technique which seeks to overcome the possible bias in the group from a few strong (or several weak) individuals.

Each member of the group is asked to spend a period of time (say, ten minutes) recording a list of risks. Then each in turn briefly presents one risk for the group's consideration. The group discusses each risk with the aim of summarising in a standard form – typically, a risk title, a risk owner and, sometimes, a brief risk description. As each risk is introduced and discussed, duplicates and associated material can be removed from the participants' original lists. This continues until the unique material from each of the original lists has been discussed.

The NGT is often extended to include risk scoring. This will be necessary if the list of risks is to be constrained to a predetermined maximum number in order to focus the team on the most important risks. Scoring may be conducted in a number of different ways. A simple approach is for team members to individually score risks on a numbered 'gut feel' severity scale (say, 1 to 5). The individual scores are then combined to produce a first-pass rank order. Another approach is to use a simple probability – impact scoring table and ask the group to reach a consensus for each risk.

When a rank-order approach has been used to identify the most significant risks, the final stage may be to examine whether or not the other risks can be reasonably subsumed.

This technique works well for some groups, but it can be a rather lengthy process. The facilitator needs to be able to maintain momentum by writing up risk titles and risk descriptions in a concise manner and intervening when the discussion has lost direction. In order to achieve this the facilitator might choose to preclude any discussion beyond points of clarification, but this has the disadvantage of losing some of the interactivity between individuals, which is such a valuable component of a group technique. The other problem that can arise following a NGT session is that the simplified techniques used for risk rank ordering are both crude and difficult to repeat. Participants should thus be aware that the primary purpose of the session is risk identification, and that the more in-depth assessment that will follow should be expected to produce changes.

A2 QUALITATIVE ASSESSMENT TECHNIQUES

A2.1 Risk descriptions/meta-language

The essence of qualitative risk assessment is that it should lead to the identification of effective actions for risk management. Since the most effective actions are usually proactive approaches that address the risk at source, the primary purpose of qualitative risk assessment should be to gain an under-standing of the source of each risk. The techniques described below show how a structured approach to the development of risk descriptions helps to achieve this aim.

The top half of Figure A.5 illustrates a general structure for the mechanism of a risk. It shows that there will be circumstances in the project or its envi-ronment that cause it to be exposed to risk. These circumstances can be expressed as statements of fact and are inherent to the project definition and baseline as expressed by its objectives and plans. The dotted arrow leading to the 'Effects' box shows that there may be uncertainty as to whether or not the risk will occur. The probability of occurrence is influenced by the nature of the uncertain events with which the risk is associated. The same and/or other uncertainties may also influence the extent of the effects that occur. The source of each risk concerns the way uncertain events are related to the underlying circumstances.

The most important point to emerge from Figure A.5 is that, in order for the risk to be addressed at source, mitigation actions should be devel-oped from an understanding of the underlying circumstances and the

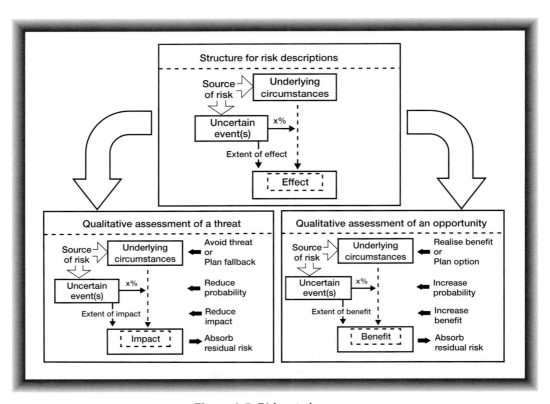

Figure A.5 *Risk meta-language*

uncertain events. The bottom of the figure shows how proactive actions (those with arrows pointing to the left) can be used to manage both threats and opportunities.

However, the planning implications often make it difficult to change the underlying circumstances. For example, alternative solutions may be available as fallbacks, but the consequences of adopting them might make them unattractive. Similarly, altering underlying circumstances by changing the project objectives may be unacceptable to stakeholders. In practice, therefore, the preferred options for risk mitigation are usually those that improve the outlook for the risk probability or extent of effect. In order to be able to identify such options, it is necessary to understand the nature of uncertain events so that they can be managed proactively to the project's advantage.

Understanding the nature of uncertain events usually requires some lateral thinking. Since mitigation actions should be related closely to such events and the reasons why they are uncertain, it may be intuitively easier to understand them by considering the effect of the actions that could be used to manage them. For example, if a project manager is concerned about a risk for which the underlying circumstances and potential effects are obvious, he or she might be able to understand the uncertain events by asking 'What could I do that would make the difference as to whether or not this risk occurs?'.

Use of an appropriate meta-language can aid the capture of a risk description consistent with the risk assessment structure illustrated in Figure A.5. Meta-language uses words or symbols to structure thinking and describe a concept in a systematic and formal way. Risk meta-language uses a three-part structured description of a risk. Requiring each element to be explicitly stated using precise words minimises confusion between the three parts – for example:

'As a result of <statement of fact>, <uncertain event(s)> may occur, which would lead to <effect on objective(s)>.'

Risk practitioners have introduced variations on this theme whilst maintaining the same three-part structure. For example, the second part might be written 'If <uncertain event(s)>' or '<uncertain event(s)> could influence'. In practice, some risks may lend themselves more naturally to one form of words than another.

A2.2 Influence diagrams

Influence diagrams are a technique that can be used as an aid to root source risk identification, qualitative analysis and quantitative analysis. The technique is most powerful when the succession of all three is used. This section will look at why influence diagrams should be used in certain circumstances, and will then look at their use in identification, qualitative analysis and quantitative analysis.

A2.2.1 Why use influence diagrams?

Most projects using risk management are likely to maintain a project risk register (PRR). This plays two important roles: as a formal repository for knowledge concerning risk events, and as the foundation for the analysis and management that flows from this knowledge.

However, the use of the PRR in these roles is too frequently predicated on the assumption that risks are independent of each other. This is rarely the case – some risks will be directly implied by other risks (and, indeed, there might be whole cascades of implied risks), and some risks will be more subtly interconnected (for example, the risk of an unsuccessful engine development and that of an unsuccessful gearbox development might both depend on the risk of an inadequate definition phase). Furthermore, the impacts from some risks might compound the impact of others, so that the effect of two risks might be more than the sum of the two individual risk effects. Some interconnections between risks might lead to positive feedback loops ('vicious circles' for threats or 'virtuous circles' for opportunities). Even the most sophisticated database tools currently available for maintaining PRRs are limited in their ability to support the analysis of this data. Although such tools may contain some relevant fields such as those that record associated risks, correlations and secondary impacts, their vertical structures tend to make such information difficult to use and inefficient to maintain. These limitations may become particularly important on complex projects.

The use of the PRR also assumes that the main risks have all been included. The techniques described in Section A1 facilitate the generation of risks. In addition, the risk description/meta-language technique described in Section A2.1 provides a structured approach to describing the source of risks. Influence diagrams extend these principles by helping to stimulate thinking about the way in which complex risks can be traced back to their root source and by identifying systemic risk structures.

A2.2.2 What are influence diagrams?

A good technique used to interview managers and subsequently model their explanations for situations in a wide variety of domains is that known as cognitive mapping. This technique structures the way in which humans construe and make sense of their experiences by developing a map consisting of elements, or concepts, joined by links showing relationships between elements. This is a useful technique to help elicit the underlying structure of causes in a 'messy' problem and results in a 'cognitive map' of the various causes and effects, with arrows or lines showing interrelationships between the elements. Where the concepts are sufficiently well defined, and the links between them can all be given a direction of causality (so that A → B means not simply that they are 'related in some way' but A is a cause or promoter of B), then we have a 'cause map' or (more loosely) an

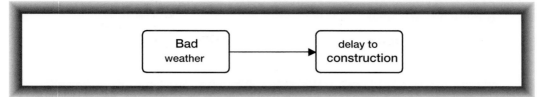

Figure A.6 *The risk of 'bad weather' increases the risk of delays to construction*

'influence diagram'. The maps are drawn simply as concepts in boxes, linked with arrows showing the direction of causality, as shown by the example in Figure A.6.

A2.2.3 Using influence diagrams for identification

Using this mapping technique will prompt the user to ask questions such as 'What could cause this risk to happen?' (to move backwards in chains of causality) and 'What would happen/what would be more likely to happen if this risk occurred?' in order to draw up the chains of causality and thus construct the causal map.

The act of drawing up a cause map of the risks, rather than listing them in a PRR, gives a number of benefits. The use of a cause-mapping technique, aided by appropriate software, is a powerful means of drawing out knowledge of project risk. It enhances clarity of thought as duplications, contradictions and inconsistencies are revealed or highlighted; it allows investigation of the interactions between risks; and it helps to 'spark off' new thoughts on risks and their relationships. As well as individuals, it can also help groups. A well-defined, methodologically sound facilitation process delivered by a trained facilitator, particularly when using visualisation software, brings out interactions between the managers, helps to surface cultural differences and helps different people to contribute different knowledge, thus giving rise to a richer set of knowledge.

A2.2.4 Qualitative analysis

The map will help analyse the risks qualitatively in a number of ways.

First, simply by drawing up the map and thinking about the contents, the knock-on effects of risks will be included in the considerations. Often, the combination of effects can become more than the sum of its parts (called 'the portfolio effect', or '2+2=5'). For example, a number of small delays in a North Sea oil-platform project can cause a project to miss a weather-window and cause significant delay. In some examples the portfolio effect is not so obvious: for instance, as when a succession of project change orders on a project collide and, as management try to deal with them, their effects compound each other.

Using appropriate software can considerably enhance the information available. Display functions in software enable concepts to be shown in different colours or shapes, categorised (for example) by uncertainty level, or impact level. Similarly, the dispersion of the risk can be explored by categorising risks for the different elements of the project visually. Appropriate software also gives the ability to see both the 'big picture' (leading towards overall project risk) and the detail (for example, risk events), particularly where there are many elements to the project.

Analysis facilities within software enable users to carry out a number of analysis functions. Most important is the identification of feedback loops which represent the most problematic way in which effects can combine. A causal chain where Risk A causes or exacerbates Risk B, which causes or exacerbates Risk C and so on can generally be easily captured by standard methods. However, where Risk C also leads back to Risk A, this gives a feedback loop. If the loop is positive, each effect tends to increase itself and the project spirals (these are called 'vicious circles' if the effect is unwanted, or 'virtuous circles' if the effect is positive), the '2+2=5' effect can often become a '2+2=6, 7 or even 8' effect, as effects interact on each other and a vicious/virtuous circle.

As well as identifying loops, other analysis facilities will help exploration of chains of causality, identification of particular problematic areas (risks which cause many consequences or problem areas that could be caused by many risks), and exploration of the effects that preventive and corrective actions might have on the whole project.

The key qualitative analyses, then, are exploring the chains of causality and, in particular, identifying positive feedback loops which have the potential to produce unexpected and sometimes catastrophic effects.

A2.2.5 Quantitative analysis

If structures of causality have been found, it is very important that these are included in the analysis; treating risks as independent will give quite incorrect results.

If the structures of causality found are simple, these can be analysed by the Monte Carlo methods described in Sections A3.3. to A3.5. The only requirement is to ensure that the rules for determining whether a risk occurs or not, rather than being an independent randomly occurring event, include the relationships with other factors. Software products that include this functionality are available.

Feedback loops revealed by the qualitative analysis are more difficult to model quantitatively, although it is important to do so as they can have profound, even catastrophic, effects on project behaviour. Management scientists use a technique known as system dynamics, which models a

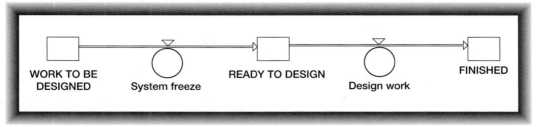

Figure A.7 *A simple model of the design stages of a project*

project as 'stocks' and 'flows' and then imposes the causality structures found in the qualitative phase on the stock/flow model to determine any changes in its behaviour. Figure A.7, based on a project to carry out design work, illustrates (albeit simplistically) what such models look like.

Figure A.7 shows a flow of work from an initial stock, which, when ready, designers will use to continue the design until it is finished. If, suppose, there is a risk that a law associated with the product will change (for example, on environmental or safety law), this may inhibit the ability to freeze the design and/or require some work to be redone. Accordingly, the model would be modified to that shown in Figure A.8.

A fuller explanation of system dynamics is outside the scope of this *Guide*, but it can be very useful where the effects of feedback loops – which can be both counterintuitive and severe – need to be quantified.

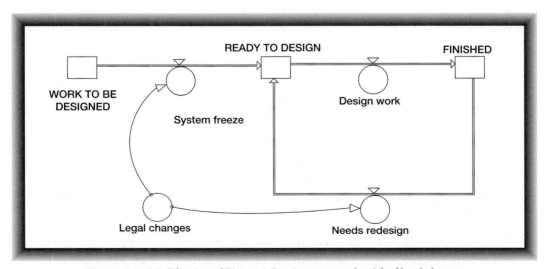

Figure A.8 *Modification of Figure A.7 to incorporate the risk of legal changes*

A2.3 Probability-impact scores

The processes of risk identification and qualitative assessment result in a number of risks, each of which poses a threat or an opportunity to the project objectives. If there are a large number of risks it is usually necessary to rank them in order of significance. In this way, the project team will be able to address those risks that have most impact, as a priority. One technique for ranking risks is to use a scoring system based on probability and impact. Although this technique has significant limitations, it has the advantage of being both simple and easy to build into a risk database tool.

A risk's probability may be classified using an agreed scale. The most common approaches are to use either a three-band (HI, MED and LO) or five-band (VHI, HI, MED, LO and VLO) scale to convert the percentage probability of occurrence into a significance level. Values typically chosen for a five-band scale are shown in the two left-hand side columns of Table A.2.

In the case of a risk that is a threat to the project's objectives, the effect of the risk's occurrence could include impact on the project schedule, costs or the performance of its product. Table A.2 shows possible criteria for classifying impact into a five-band scale. Tables of this type are usually referred to as a risk criteria table. It would be possible to classify opportunity benefits in a similar manner.

Table A.2 Example of a risk criteria and scores table

Scale	Probability of Occurrence		Impact on Project			
	Probability	Probability score	Project schedule	Project cost	Product performance	Impact score
VLO	<10%	0.1	<2 weeks	<1%	Temporary defects, causing minor short-term consequences	0.05
LO	10% – <30%	0.3	2 weeks – <1 month	1% – <2%	Product performance shortfall in area of tertiary (or minor) importance	0.1
MED	30% – <50%	0.5	1 month – <2 months	2% – <4%	Product performance shortfall in area of secondary importance	0.2
HI	50% – <70%	0.7	2 month – <4 months	4% – <8%	Minor product performance shortfall in area of critical (or primary purpose)	0.4
VHI	70% +	0.9	4 months +	8% +	Significant failure of product to meet one of its critical (or primary) purposes.	0.8

Having classified the probability and impact of each risk, it is then possible to allocate a score for each probability and impact band. Table A.2 shows a commonly used scheme for these scores. It should be noted that the probability scores for this scheme are defined using a linear arithmetical scale, whereas the impact scores are on a logarithmic scale. This is consistent with the scales used for criteria definitions.

It should be noted that, depending on the nature of the project, other aspects of impact might be equally relevant, or even more relevant, than product performance. Examples could include market penetration or disruption to operations. The criteria table should therefore be constructed to reflect the critical success criteria for the project. The scales used should also be tailored to the project and agreed with all relevant stakeholders. The borderline between very high- and high-impact threats is often drawn on the basis that the occurrence of a very high-impact threat would be simply unacceptable and a very high-impact opportunity too good to leave to chance.

A rank-order index can be calculated by multiplying the risk scores for the probability and overall impact of each risk. The overall impact score should normally be equal to whichever of the impacts from amongst the three or more impact categories has the highest value. Some ranking schemes may be based on an overall impact as the sum of three impact scores. However, this is not to be recommended. If the very high impact of a threat is by definition unacceptable, it should be ranked as being of high priority even if it has an impact in only one dimension.

The matrix in Figure A.9 shows the possible probability-impact ranking index values for the threats classified by Table A.2. The shaded areas represent the index values for the highest priority risks.

Probability						
0.9	VHI	0.045	0.09	0.18	0.36	0.72
0.7	HI	0.035	0.07	0.14	0.28	0.56
0.5	MED	0.025	0.05	0.10	0.20	0.40
0.3	LO	0.015	0.03	0.06	0.12	0.24
0.1	VLO	0.005	0.01	0.02	0.04	0.08
		VLO	LO	MED	HI	VHI
		0.05	0.1	0.2	0.4	0.8
		Impact				

Figure A.9 *Example of probability-impact ranking index values*

143

As can be seen from the figure, the ranking priority order for risks is weighted towards impact rather than probability. Thus, a very high-impact/very low-probability risk is considered to be of more concern than a very low-impact/very high-probability risk. This weighting is likely to be appropriate to most projects, since the high impacts are often disproportionately severe in comparison with low impacts, and because the highest impact band in any scale is usually classified as having no upper limit. Nevertheless, there may be projects for which probability should be of equal, or greater, weight, such as those that are exposed to the frequent occurrence of risks that have relatively predictable and minor consequences.

			Threats				Arrow of attention		Opportunities					
0.9	VHI	0.045	0.09	0.18	0.36	0.72	0.72	0.36	0.18	0.09	0.045	0.9	VHI
0.7	HI	0.035	0.07	0.14	0.28	0.56	0.56	0.28	0.14	0.07	0.035	0.7	HI
0.5	MED	0.025	0.05	0.10	0.20	0.40	0.40	0.20	0.10	0.05	0.025	0.5	MED
0.3	LO	0.015	0.03	0.06	0.12	0.24	0.24	0.12	0.06	0.03	0.015	0.3	LO
0.1	VLO	0.005	0.01	0.02	0.04	0.08	0.08	0.04	0.02	0.01	0.005	0.1	VLO
		VLO	LO	MED	HI	VHI	VHI	HI	MED	LO	VLO		
		0.05	0.1	0.2	0.4	0.8	0.8	0.4	0.2	0.1	0.05		
				Impact					Benefit				

Probability (left axis) / Probability (right axis)

Figure A.10 *Example of a combined risk-ranking scheme for threats and opportunities*

It is possible to extend the principles described so far in this section to a combined ranking for threats and opportunities. Figure A.10 shows a mirror-imaged scheme that achieves this. In this figure, risks within the top-right area of the threats region and the top-left area of the opportunities region form an 'arrow of attention' for risk management.

A2.3.1 Using probability-impact scores for risk reporting and monitoring

Ranking risks by using probability-impact scores can be combined with other risk classification data to produce usefully focused reports. For example, it may be possible to interrogate a risk database with instructions such as 'List the Top 5 risks associated with the delivery of [a named milestone]' or 'What are the Top 10 schedule risks?'. One of the advantages of using a risk database tool for maintaining a risk register is the ability to sort information in this fashion. Typical key fields for filtering and sorting include risk owner, risk type, risk trigger date, WBS code, and owning organisation.

A P-I matrix may also provide a graphical means of presenting risk data. For example, it may be possible to list risks in a P-I grid using different colours for different risk types. This form of report would indicate which types of risk were those of the greatest number and/or consequence. A similar approach can be taken to the illustration of risk trends. Using different colours (or arrows to show direction of change) for risk assessments made at different points in time may help to show whether or not risk exposures are deteriorating or improving.

A2.3.2 Limitations of probability-impact scores

Probability-impact scoring processes of the type described in this section have two very important strengths. The first is that they are relatively easy for all project personnel to use and understand; the second is that they can be readily built into the functionality of risk database. However, the technique is so widely used that its limitations are often overlooked. The following points are therefore worth bearing in mind:

1 The scoring process produces a relatively crude technique for ranking. Since risks are categorised using bands, there are significant areas of overlap in risk exposure between adjacent boxes in the grid. The 3×3 matrix approach is particularly crude and is only recommended for smaller projects, or for a first-pass assessment.
2 The technique is appropriate to risks that have a probability of occurrence of less than 100 per cent. Risks that are purely concerned with outcome variance (for example, the duration uncertainty for a design activity) could present themselves in this format as either a threat or an opportunity, depending on the planned target. As a first pass, risks of this nature would be better ranked using a measure of uncertainty such as the width of their probability distribution function.
3 The index numbers are designed only to rank risks, and therefore have no absolute meaning. It is not meaningful to add these numbers to obtain 'total project scores' to compare project solutions or monitor trends.
4 The action of multiplying the probability and consequence scores to produce the ranking index does not always produce a preferred rank order. The most common case for making an exception is that of the very high-impact/very low-probability threat, for which many projects will choose to assign a higher index value.
5 The project may adopt a different prioritisation strategy for threats as compared to opportunities. For example, after project approval, stakeholders may be less inclined to try to exploit low-probability opportunities. This might lead to a rank-order shift away from impacts towards probabilities for opportunities.

It should be noted that the quantitative risk analysis techniques described later in this appendix provide alternative approaches to rank-order prioritisation. Techniques such as sensitivity analysis, criticality analysis, tornado graphs and the schedule sensitivity index (all described later in this appendix) also have the advantage of evaluating risks more closely to the context of overall project risk. Projects that invest in the use of such quantitative techniques will therefore have a choice. Typically, the qualitative ranking process may be employed for routine risk control whilst quantitative ranking data will be available at strategic points in the project.

A2.4 Risk registers and databases

A risk register provides a structured approach to recording risk data and generating reports. It is possible to use a very simple tool, such as a spreadsheet, to maintain data in a risk register but if more than a minimal number of fields are used, it usually becomes more economical to employ a database application, as described in Chapter 8.

The level of detail that it is appropriate to maintain can vary considerably from one project to another. For very simple projects, or for the first pass of the risk management process, it may be appropriate to restrict the risk register to the minimal number of fields shown in Table A.3. However, for more complex projects, or as more information becomes known, data fields have to be added in order to be able to focus, analyse and sort the data for different purposes. The second column of Table A.3 shows the data fields that might be used for a typical project team in which there is a formal risk management function and the third column illustrates ways in which these might be expanded to compile a very detailed risk register.

Although there is always a case that can be made for adding any individual data field, projects should be mindful of the trade-offs to be made between detail and the practicalities of data maintenance. For example, if all of the data fields listed in the third column of Table A.3 were used, a risk for which there were five mitigation actions could end up with almost 100 data entries. The effort required to maintain such levels of detailed data fresh is likely to be a threat to either other project activities or the willingness of team members to engage actively in the risk management process. The project should therefore take care to understand how risk data will be reviewed, reported and acted upon before defining the fields to be maintained in its risk register. Data fields that make little or no contribution to the project's decision-making processes should be omitted.

A3 QUANTITATIVE TECHNIQUES

A3.1 Three-point estimates

Most quantitative risk analysis techniques are based on the assumption that it is possible to estimate a continuous probability distribution function for the outcome of a planned element of the project or the outcome of a risk event (should the risk occur). Cost and duration are the parameters that are most commonly used for analysis, but similar approaches can sometimes be

Table A.3 Examples of risk registers at different levels of detail

Minimalist Risk Register	Typical Risk Register	Detailed Risk Register
Risk ID	Risk ID	Risk ID
Risk Title	Risk Title	Risk Title
N/A	Risk Status (Open, Closed etc.)	Risk Status
Risk Owner	Risk Owner	Risk Owner
		(Impacts on) Interested Parties
	Risk-Owning Organisation	Risk-Owning Organisation
		Risk Share % (by organisation)
N/A	Project Area	WBS/PBS/OBS Reference(s)
		Other User-definable Fields
Risk Description	Risk Type	Risk Type
	Risk Background	Risk Background
	Potential Causes	Potential Causes
		Risk Trigger date(s)
		Estimating Notes for probability
		Secondary Risk Triggers
	Risk Consequences	Risk Consequences
		Estimating Notes for calculation of schedule and cost impact values
		Risk Impact Start and Finish dates
		Secondary Risk Consequences
N/A	Associated Risks	Associated Risks
		Parent Risks
Probability (recorded as single value, e.g. Hi, Med, Low etc)	Probability %	Pre-risk Response Probability %
		Post-risk Response Probability %
Impacts recorded separately as single values (e.g. Hi, Med, Low)	Schedule Impact Three-point Estimate	Schedule Impact Three-Point Estimates (Pre- and Post-Response)
– Schedule	Cost Impact Three-point Estimate	Cost Impact Three-Point Estimates (Pre- and Post-Response)
– Cost		
– Product Performance	Product Impact (recorded as single value, e.g. VHI–VLow)	Product Impact (Pre- and Post-Response)
	Other Impact Categories (as agreed in impact criteria table)	Other Impact Categories (Pre- and Post-Response)
Risk Response Strategy	Risk Response Strategy	Risk Response Strategy
	Response Actions, each with:	Response Actions, each with:
	– Action Description	– Action Description
	– Action Owner	– Action Owner
	– Action Status	– Action Status
	– Action Start Date	– Action Start Date
	– Planned Completion Date	– Planned Completion Date
		– Action Cost
		– Project Planning ref. for action
N/A	Fallback(s)	Fallback Plans, each with:
		– Fallback Description
		– Cost Impact
		– Schedule Impact
		– Fallback Decision Date
N/A	Date of Most Recent Review	Date of Most Recent Review
	Historical Notes (review dates and significant changes)	Automated Recording of all Reviews and all Changes to the Risk Register
		Risk identified by:
		– Individual, Team or Organisation
		– Date Identified

used for the analysis of a product, particularly if product outcome can be measured in a single dimension.

A common technique for defining probability distributions is to decide on an appropriate distribution shape and to make a three-point estimate which defines the spread of possible outcomes as follows:

- low value
- most likely value (mode)
- high value.

Whilst it is not easy to make realistic three-point estimates, a good estimating strategy makes realistic estimates much more likely. Typically, immature processes produce three-point estimates that are too narrow and either pessimistically or (more commonly) optimistically biased. Since the quality of quantitative analysis is dependent on the validity of the estimates, it is important to use a robust estimating strategy. The following notes provide guidance on the factors that should be taken into account.

1 **The estimator must understand the implications of the probability distribution shape**.

    Figure A.11 shows three of the most common probability distributions used and illustrates their shape with a negative skew that is typical for project activities. It is good practice to provide the estimator with diagrams such as these so that he or she can appreciate both the nature of the shape and the significance of the three estimating points.

    When using the triangular or Beta PERT distributions, the low and high estimates represent the extreme values of possible outcome, so the spread of the three-point estimate should be appropriately broad. When using the general triangular distribution, the low and high estimates represent cumulative percentile points on the probability distribution. Three-point estimates made on this basis should be correspondingly narrower.

2 **The estimator should consider all relevant sources of uncertainty**.

    Three-point estimates that are too narrow are often the result of thinking through the implications of a narrow range of issues whilst failing to question key assumptions or consider how uncertainties could combine. The following are all typical sources of uncertainty that influence variance in outcome:

    - productivity rates and resourcing assumptions
    - definition and interpretation of the scope of work
    - variations in required quantities (for example, the number of lines of software code)
    - project management effectiveness
    - scope for omissions, duplications and mistakes
    - accuracy of estimating metrics
    - willingness of suppliers to be realistic about forecasts
    - validity of labour escalation and material cost assumptions
    - management priorities.

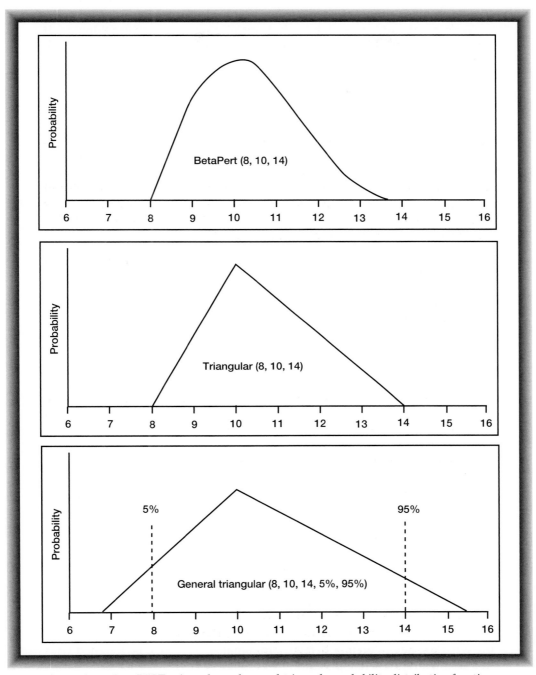

Figure A.11 *Beta PERT, triangular and general triangular probability distribution functions*

Outcomes that tend towards the extreme may arise from scenarios in which assumptions are violated and uncertainties combine. Estimating a realistic spread is therefore likely to require some contingent thinking. It is good practice to record a rationale for the high and low values.

3 **The estimator should follow a process designed to avoid bias and unrealistically low outcome variance.**
    The following process is recommended to overcome these problems:
    - List all uncertainty factors that are likely to affect outcome variance.
    - Make the high-value (pessimistic) estimate first.
    - Make the low-value (optimistic) estimate second.
    - Record the rationale for the high and low values.
    - Make the most likely estimate.
    - Identify and record the reasons for differences between the most likely estimate and the planned value, or adjust the planned value to that of the most likely estimate.

4 **The estimator should avoid assuming that the most likely value is equal to that which has been planned.**
    Making such an assumption is a common cause for the presence of bias in three-point estimates. For example, if the planned value is based on an aggressive target, a realistic estimate for the most likely value is likely to be higher. In contrast, if the planned value is based on a commitment to which there is a high level of confidence, the most likely value may realistically be lower.
    In making these comments, the *Guide* is not seeking to suggest that target setting is poor practice or that commitments should be disregarded. It is simply emphasising that there should be a distinction between targets, commitments and estimates. Indeed, one of the benefits of the risk management process should be that these distinctions are understood and recorded.

5 **Organisations and projects should maintain data to compare actual outcomes with the three-point estimates that were made for them.**
    This can be applied to overall project risk or outcomes of individual activities. Practice has shown that organisations that monitor their performance in this way are able to improve the quality of their risk estimates.

A3.2 Simple quantitative risk models

Using an iterative (multiple-pass) approach is fundamental to the effective use of the PRAM approach to quantitative risk management model building. The first pass is usually concerned with the aspects of uncertainty that matter most – where the key threats and opportunities lie. This means that the first pass should focus on sizing uncertainty, with further passes exploring what matters in greater detail. A 'minimalist' approach is designed with this simple first-pass role in mind.

Each risk event probability and its associated impact can be sized in terms of two estimates, a 'minimum' and a 'maximum'. Each minimum can be interpreted as a plausible 10 percentile value, and each maximum can be interpreted as a plausible 90 percentile value, using simple rounded values. This avoids difficulties associated with the meaning of absolute values in a simple robust manner.

Each pair of minimum and maximum values can be associated with a uniform probability distribution (equal likelihood of any value over its range), and 80 per cent of the range can be defined by the minimum and the maximum, adding another 10 per cent at each end (see Figure A.12). The uniform distribution is conservative as well as simple, with an expected value defined by the midpoint, equal to the median (50 per cent value).

The simplest feasible level of risk event structure might be used on the first pass, but this need not be the case. For example, a schedule risk model might have a simple basic PERT model structure, with one risk event (activity duration variability) for each activity.

A Monte Carlo simulation tool can be used to combine all the risk events assuming:

- a simple form of perfect positive correlation,
- statistical independence,
- a plausible intermediate level of dependence.

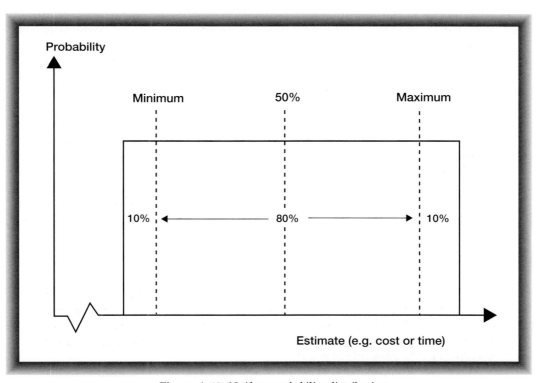

Figure A.12 *Uniform probability distribution*

It may be possible to calculate the uncertainty results from a model based on perfect (100 per cent) correlation arithmetically, but the results would normally be unrealistically wide. Conversely, assuming that each risk or activity is independent would produce a result that was too narrow, unless the model uses a very low number of estimates. However, since the main aim is to identify what matters most, the uncertainty spread in the results might not be important. If no information about dependence is available, 50 per cent dependence is a plausible midpoint estimate. However, mature processes will usually employ alternatives. For example, when costing oil refineries in the 1980s, based on empirical studies, BP adopted 75 per cent as a plausible level for simple sum of cost item variability estimates.

It is useful to structure the simulation so that cumulative probability curves, like those of Figure 4.3 (p. 37), show how the uncertainty builds, as risk events are combined, presenting the overall outcome. When it is clear which risk events are the major contributors to project risk, later passes can develop more clarity in the areas that are found to matter most.

Several different lines of model development may need to be considered and used. Some risk events may be worth decomposing into simple terms. For example, activity variations defined as a single risk event in a basic PERT model might be decomposed into 'normal variations' and 'abnormal variations', with illustrations of each drawn from the risk register. Other risk events may be worth more complex decomposition. For example, 'abnormal variations' might be decomposed into 'major equipment failures', 'extremely good weather', 'extremely bad weather' and so on. Within each of these different levels of risk event decomposition, the modelling can use the simple uniform probability distribution approach or it can employ three-point estimates and other refinements discussed below. Further, dependence can be treated with related levels of complexity, using conditional specifications (as used in decision trees) and causal models that decompose the structure of event risks and responses until statistical independence is a credible assumption.

A3.3 Monte Carlo analysis

Monte Carlo analysis is a widely used and powerful quantitative risk analysis technique. The most common subjects for Monte Carlo analysis are overall project cost and time. The same principles can sometimes also be applied to product outcome, particularly if the key features of the project's product can be measured in with a single dimension. The results can therefore be interpreted from the perspective of overall project risk. A key feature of the technique is that it offers an approach that combines the assessment of individual risk events with an analysis that concerns overall project risk, thus integrating the two definitions of the word 'risk' that are used by this *Guide* (see p. 17).

However, Monte Carlo simulation is also a technique that demands significant time, effort, judgement and skill. When used well, Monte Carlo analysis adds value to the management of projects, but if it is used inappropriately it may deliver dangerously misleading information.

Figure A.13 is a generic illustration of the way in which Monte Carlo analysis is used. The simulation process – in which input values are chosen randomly from within probability distributions and then combined and calculated as simulated outputs – is a mechanistic one that can be handled efficiently by modern software tools. In contrast, the issues that affect the quality of analysis are associated with the points in the process at which there is human intervention – namely:

● the risk estimates
● the Monte Carlo model
● the way in which the results are used and interpreted.

The way in which the results are used depends on the purposes of the analysis and should be understood before the model is constructed. Similarly, there should be a good understanding of the model before the input estimates are made. Accordingly, this section deals first with the purposes of Monte Carlo analysis and then with modelling techniques. Guidance on estimating is covered in section A3.1 ('Three-Point Estimates'). It concludes

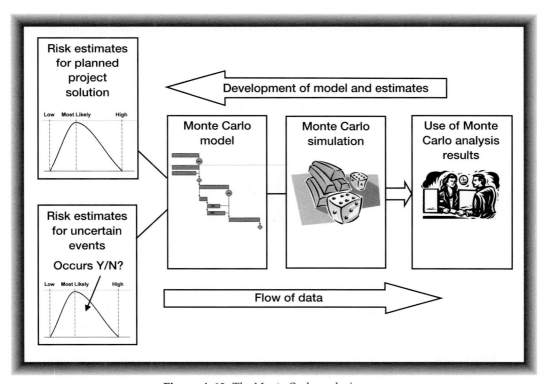

Figure A.13 *The Monte Carlo analysis process*

with a feature that should be considered for all project risk models – that of simulating the interdependencies between project activities using statistical dependencies (or correlation).

A3.3.1 The purposes of Monte Carlo analysis

In general, the purposes of a Monte Carlo analysis are to forecast a realistic probability distribution for outcome and to understand the dynamics of a project in a way that helps its management. The results may therefore be used to:

- identify the work content and risks that have the most influence on the variance of project outcome
- perform a healthcheck on the project's plans
- evaluate the scope for the use of proactive risk mitigation
- estimate the contingencies that the project requires to have a given level of confidence in achieving success
- compare the risk efficiency of alternative project solutions
- evaluate the implications of arrangements for bearing responsibility for risk
- provide evidence to stakeholders at key investment decision points.

The intended purposes of analysis and their relative importance should influence the way in which a Monte Carlo model is constructed. For example, if the primary purpose is to estimate schedule contingencies, a model will be required that includes all work that could potentially be critical (whilst avoiding the pitfalls of including too much detail) and simulates correlation between activity outcomes. On the other hand, if the primary purpose is to identify the work content and risks that have the most influence on project outcome, the use of correlation might be less important and the level of detail somewhat greater.

The ways in which the purposes of Monte Carlo analysis affect the construction of models are discussed in the paragraphs that follow for each type of model. However, before this, there are a number of other issues that should be taken into account when conducting the analysis and reporting on the results. These include recording and reporting of assumptions, the potential for bias and the natural limitations of this approach when applied to the assessment of overall project risk.

A3.3.2 Assumptions

Any Monte Carlo model will be based on assumptions, violations of which are outside the scope of modelling. For example, certain estimates might have been developed on the basis that a particular contractor would be employed or on the assumption that the priority accorded to the project would eliminate resource limitations from consideration. As Monte Carlo results are potentially misleading if the audience is unaware of significant assumptions, the risk analyst should record all of these and include them in reports.

A3.3.3 Bias

Bias is systematic error that may be optimistic or pessimistic, conscious or unconscious. If stakeholders or project team members influence the Monte Carlo analysis by providing estimates or modelling assumptions that are biased, the analysis results will be misleading. (Of course, it should be emphasised that such a bias may be present even if it has not been introduced consciously.) The cumulative effect of relatively small errors of judgement can build up to a significant gap in analysis if the errors are systematic. Such errors can be the consequence of the project planning processes and the environment in which they take place and do not necessarily require the conscious introduction of bias by individuals.

Pressure to demonstrate a high level of confidence in targets tends to produce optimistic bias. The most obvious example of this occurs when Monte Carlo analysis results are used to evaluate confidence in a project's business case, leading to a major investment decision. In this situation, a conflict of interest can develop between members of the project team, who want to be sure that the project gains approval, and stakeholders, who want to be assured of a high probability of success. Since the project team normally manages the Monte Carlo model and estimates, stakeholders should take steps to ensure that the process used to generate the model and estimates is subject to independent scrutiny.

In contrast, accountability issues may cause individuals to protect themselves by introducing a pessimistic bias. A common cause of this is previous experience of arbitrary budget cuts. Correction requires a management solution that establishes fairness and consistency. This may involve differentiating between targets (the achievement of which may require a balance towards good luck) and realistic risk estimates.

A3.3.4 Limitations

Users of Monte Carlo results should be aware of the limitations of the technique. Whilst it provides a powerful tool for analysis, it is not a complete solution to the forecasting of all project risk. In practice it may be difficult to model certain risks, including potential showstoppers or risks associated with the project environment that cannot be modelled as impacting on discrete areas of the plan.

Although obvious, it should also be remembered that Monte Carlo models do not include unidentified and unidentifiable risks.

For these reasons, Monte Carlo results should be treated intelligently and in the context of the project environment. For example, if the results are used to estimate schedule or financial contingency requirements, there should be separate allowances made for overall project risk that cannot be modelled in this way. For example, a project may maintain two budgets for financial contingencies – one to cover risk that can be identified and modelled, and another to cover its exposure to unidentified events.

A3.4 Monte Carlo schedule models

A typical Monte Carlo schedule model comprises a network of activities, risk events and milestones. The milestones are chosen as focal points of interest for the simulation results. The network of activities should be informed by the schedule that is used for the normal project planning process, although it is usually not good practice for the risk model to be a straight copy. Probability distribution functions will be estimated for each activity to simulate the variance in its duration, resources or logic. Probabilistic risk events can be simulated as additional activities whose duration is zero (should the risk not occur) or a value chosen from a probability distribution function that represents the range of possible duration should the risk occur. In certain cases, risk events may be better simulated by probabilistic or conditional branches. Probabilistic branches are formed where there is uncertainty as to whether one way of implementing the project will be used or another. Conditional

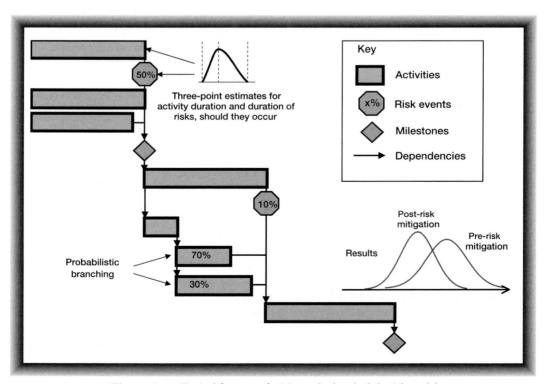

Figure A.14 *Typical features of a Monte Carlo schedule risk model*

branches are employed to simulate the use of an alternative implementation dependent on the outcome of a simulated factor – for example the use of a planned fallback should a milestone slip beyond a critical point. Figure A.14 depicts a graphical representation of the model.

As a schedule risk model is being developed, it is important to understand the level of activity detail that should be simulated. Even on very large projects and during later passes of the risk process, a good schedule risk model is unlikely to have more than 250 activities and risks, and there are usually good reasons for using a number that is very much smaller. The reasons for setting this limit are as follows:

1   Confidence in the validity of dependencies at lower levels of detail may be questionable, particularly, in the case of long-duration projects in which the schedule will evolve as the project progresses.
2   The attention that can be paid to developing good quality risk estimates will almost certainly be diminished by having to make estimates for a large number of activities.
3   Many activities on the full project schedule have no significance to a timescale risk analysis, either because there is no likelihood that they will be critical or because they simply mark out budgets for cost collection.
4   If each activity is simulated independently (that is, there is no correlation between activities) the spread of results from a model with a large number of activities becomes unrealistically narrow. This is particularly the case where activities are linked in series.

The Monte Carlo process assumes that each network dependency is 100 per cent valid. As increasing levels of granularity are introduced into the model there is therefore a danger that detail that appears to be justified on the grounds of objectivity in fact becomes irrational. This means that there is therefore a trade-off to be made between the aim of using the model to understand details within the project schedule and the aim of producing a realistic forecast of schedule variance. Detail should only be increased where there is a high level of confidence in the validity of dependencies and where the detail leads to better estimates and/or understanding of the schedule dynamics.

After having understood the purposes of the analysis, the first step towards constructing a Monte Carlo schedule model is to choose the milestones to be simulated. The criteria used to select these milestones should be that:

● they are key subjects of interest for managers and stakeholders
● they can be associated with defined products or events
● they are spread relatively evenly across time
● they bring together dependencies from parallel paths in the schedule.

The network of activities required to achieve these milestones can then be defined. On a first-pass model, this network is likely to provide a coarse level of detail as described in section A3.1 ('Simple Quantitative Risk Models'). At subsequent passes, more granularity can be added as more information starts to become available for those areas of the project schedule that are relatively exposed to risk.

Many medium to large projects control their activities with a schedule that exceeds the level of detail appropriate to a Monte Carlo risk model. Thus, whilst the full schedule should be a primary source of data for the risk model, it is not usually best practice to create the model by making a simple electronic copy, although unfortunately this is often the quickest way of performing the task. If this error is compounded by making three-point estimates on a generic basis, the analysis is likely be at best useless and at worst misleading. One of the benefits of schedule risk analysis is that it provides an opportunity for performing a healthcheck on the project schedule. To achieve this benefit, the risk analyst must be able to work closely with the schedule planners and add value by bringing the risk perspective to bear.

A3.4.1 Presenting Monte Carlo schedule analysis results

Monte Carlo analysis results are usually presented as either a histogram or a cumulative curve. Both formats allow planning baselines to be shown against the risk-based forecast. Cumulative distributions are popular for presenting results because it is easy to display the results of different modelling scenarios on the same graph. However, histograms sometimes have the advantage of making it easier to identify major risk drivers. Recipients of histogram data are also somewhat less inclined to overinterpret the significance of the date at whatever level of confidence they report against. The graphs shown in Figures A.15 and A.16 show results from the same analysis.

Whilst cumulative distribution graphs and histograms are useful techniques for presenting risk-based forecasts for project outcome, Monte Carlo analysis also provides data useful for a more detailed identification of schedule risk drivers. In a mature risk management process, this is likely to be the primary purpose of the analysis. The following four techniques are discussed below:

- scenario comparisons
- criticality analysis
- schedule sensitivity index
- cruciality analysis.

A3.4.2 Scenario comparisons

Once a Monte Carlo risk model has been established, it is often possible to perform the analysis to simulate different scenarios. For example, it might be possible to avoid certain risks by making changes to the project solution. A comparison between the S-curves generated by the simulation of different scenarios would then provide an assessment of the relative merits of the

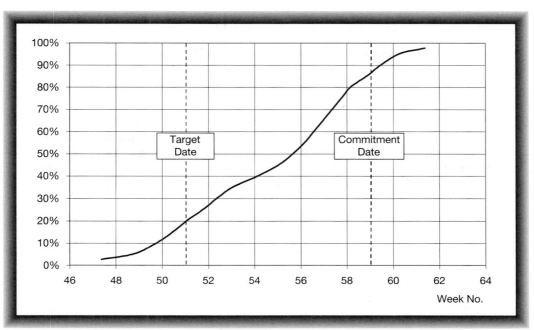

Figure A.15 *Cumulative distribution graph for milestone completion*

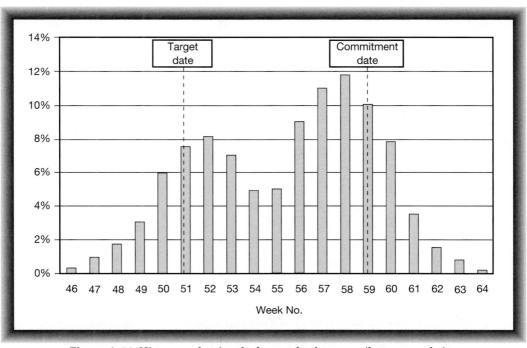

Figure A.16 *Histogram showing the forecast for the same milestone completion*

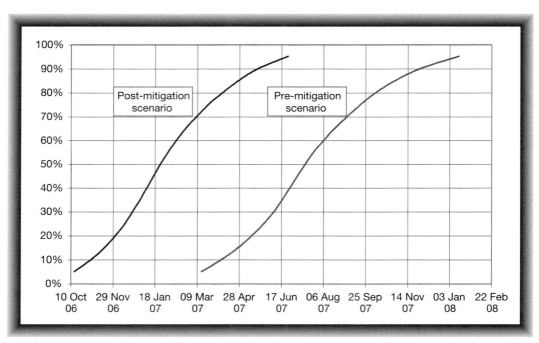

Figure A.17 *Forecasts for pre- and post-mitigation scenarios*

solutions concerned. This approach to modelling is consistent with the guidance on establishing risk-efficient solutions given in Chapter 4.

Another form of scenario comparison concerns the modelling of outcome on the basis of pre-mitigation and post-mitigation estimates. Figure A.17 shows two S-curves representing the pre- and post-mitigation scenarios. The gap between the two curves can be interpreted as being an estimate of the schedule benefit that is expected to be gained from the implementation of plans for risk mitigation (provided that the risk mitigation actions are actually implemented as planned).

A3.4.3 Criticality analysis

Criticality is defined as the percentage of simulation iterations in which an activity or risk event lies on the schedule critical path. It is therefore a measure of the probability that the activity or risk event has a direct effect on the schedule outcome. Most Monte Carlo schedule analysis tools are able to output criticality listings for activities, but a number of tools are not capable of doing this correctly for risk events (a risk event should not have a criticality greater than its probability of occurrence – that is, if it only happens half of the time, and it is always critical when it does, its criticality should be 50 per cent).

One way of identifying those elements of the schedule that have the most influence on the project duration is to list activities and risk events in a criticality rank order. This is a useful first-pass approach to using the output of the analysis to focus on schedule improvement. Its limitation is that it takes no account of the effect of activities and risk events on the variance of outcome, although this can be overcome by using the schedule sensitivity index technique described below.

A3.4.4 Schedule sensitivity index

As a measure of uncertainty, variance can be interpreted as being a reflection of a possible opportunity to improve schedule performance should the source of uncertainty be actively managed. Most Monte Carlo analysis tools are capable of monitoring the variance (and hence standard deviation) of each activity and risk event. Combining this data with criticality data allows the calculation of a schedule sensitivity index (SSI) as follows:

$$\text{SSI} = \frac{\text{Standard deviation for duration of activity (or risk event)} \times \text{Criticality}}{\text{Standard deviation of overall schedule duration}}$$

The standard deviation for the overall schedule is usually higher than the standard deviation for any activity or risk and is included as a normalisation factor that limits SSIs to a maximum value of 100 per cent. It can be noted that the calculation of SSIs is analogous to calculating Probability-Impact (P-I) values for risk events, since criticality and standard deviation may be considered as being analogous to probability and impact respectively. Like P-I values, SSIs are dimensionless numbers that do not have a meaning in themselves, but are, rather, an approach to rank ordering. Rank ordering of activities and risks using SSIs has been proved to be a simple and effective approach to the identification of the key schedule drivers, whose management is likely to yield the greatest benefit to schedule outcome.

A3.4.5 Cruciality

A number of Monte Carlo tools are able to calculate cruciality (defined as the correlation between a task's standard deviation and that of the overall project end date). Typically, the results are displayed in a Tornado graph (see Figure A.21). Cruciality values can be used to rank risks and activities in a similar way to criticality and SSI numbers. One advantage of using this technique is that a number of tools have specially designed reports to display results. Another advantage is that cruciality measures can also be applied to other quantitative modelling techniques, whereas the SSI technique is only applicable to schedule risk analysis. The chief disadvantage of cruciality calculations is that many people do not understand the mathematics and are therefore reluctant to act on the information.

In practice, SSI and cruciality calculations from a schedule risk analysis produce similar rank-order listings. Both are a significant improvement on criticality calculations.

A3.5 Monte Carlo cost models

The structure of a Monte Carlo cost model should be designed to simulate all sources of cost variance whilst avoiding the problem of double-counting which would result if the simulation of their effects was duplicated. Typically, risks might materialise as project costs in the following three different ways:

- variance of costs attributable to budget uncertainties in planned tasks
- cost consequence of risk events that might or might not occur
- variance of costs attributable to schedule variance.

In order to avoid double-counting, it is necessary to differentiate between these (or similar) effects when making risk estimates. Figure A.18 shows how a model might appear once such differentiation has been achieved. The right-hand column shows possible values for each line item during a single

| | Prob (%) | Three - point Estimates (£K) | | | Simulated Values |
		Low	ML	High	
Budget uncertainties					
Planned Task 1	N/A	−50	0	100	41.6
Planned Task 2 etc.	N/A	−100	20	280	−80.2
Potential risk events					
Risk A	25%	10	40	90	0
Risk B etc.	10%	15	20	40	17.8
Time / cost variances					
Variance X	N/A	−10	30	90	36.5
Variance Y etc.	N/A	0	20	40	17.8
N/A – Not applicable				Simulated total	33.5

Figure A.18 *Monte Carlo cost model showing simulated values during a single iteration*

iteration of a Monte Carlo simulation. The Monte Carlo model output is obtained by monitoring the simulated total for all line items shown at the bottom right.

Budget uncertainties concern the accuracy with which cost estimates can be made for the outcome of planned tasks. They can be modelled using a continuous probability distribution. The risk factors involved might include the validity of estimating metrics and variance from the assumptions used to estimate resource requirements. In contrast, the cost consequences of risk events that might or might not occur should be modelled as variable 'step changes' to the cost outcome. The step changes would result from the risk's occurrence, so within the cost model such events should be assigned a value for probability.

The greatest challenge in constructing a Monte Carlo cost model often lies in differentiating between the direct cost of risk events and the implications that schedule variance has on costs. There are usually a number of ways in which a project's costs may be increased as a function of time. The most common example is that of the 'marching army' of project support personnel (including the project management team). As with budget uncertainties, costs that vary as a function of time can usually be simulated with a continuous probability distribution. If the project has conducted a schedule risk analysis, combining the output from this with metrics for costs that are a function of time can provide a basis for defining the three-point estimates.

Some risk tools support a fully integrated cost/schedule approach to Monte Carlo analysis. The basis of the risk model should be a resourced schedule that allows a combination of activity logic and resource pool constraints to drive schedule analysis. With such tools the methods outlined in this *Guide* can be extended to model the combined effects of risks and uncertainties that pertain to activity duration, costs, resource rates and resource availability. This approach may be helpful if resource availability is a key driver of schedule risk. However, correlation of the various factors involved presents complex modelling problems, and the results may not provide greater insight than the schedule and cost risk analysis processes already described.

A3.5.1 Presenting Monte Carlo cost risk analysis results

Monte Carlo cost risk analysis results are usually presented in the form of a cumulative distribution graph (S-curve) or a histogram, equivalent to those used for schedule analysis. It is useful to include the value of planned baselines such as target or expected budgets and values for financial reserves. Figure A.19 shows a possible format for the presentation of cost risk analysis results using an S-curve.

The schedule scenario comparison techniques previously described in section A3.4.2 are also equally applicable to cost risk analysis. Figure 4.4 (p. 41) illustrates approaches that can be used to present information using

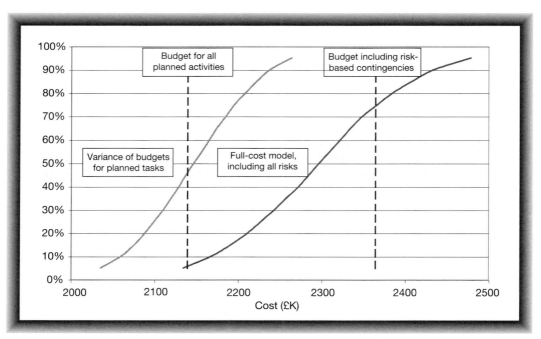

Figure A.19 *Possible presentation of the results from cost risk analysis*

cost risk analysis for different scenarios. Use of the type of presentation shown by these figures can be very helpful for the purpose of selecting risk-efficient project solutions.

A3.5.2 Simulation of statistical dependencies (correlation)

Project activities are never truly independent from one another. In practice, common factors result in a tendency for uncertainties (schedule or cost) to gravitate towards a similar region in the probability distributions that have been estimated for them. In other words, there is a positive correlation between the activity outcomes. Some common factors may pertain to the project as a whole – for example, the quality of the project management team and the robustness of the estimating process. Other common factors may be contained within certain project areas, often because they are associated with a particular group of products.

Occasionally, a negative correlation between activity outcomes might be expected. For example, if there is uncertainty as to what proportion of a certain area of the project will be subcontracted, there might be a negative correlation between the in-house and subcontract costs for the associated activities.

A Monte Carlo model should reflect the fact that activity outcomes will be correlated to some degree. Failure to do so will generate results for overall project risk that have an unrealistically small variance. This is a particular problem in Monte Carlo cost risk analysis, where the simulation is based on an arithmetic total of a large number of line items. The central limit theorem shows that if variables are simulated independently, the variance of their combined value decreases as a function of the number of variables.

Most Monte Carlo analysis tools use rank-order correlation coefficients to simulate statistical dependencies between activities. Truly independent activities would have a correlation coefficient of zero, whereas activities with a perfect positive correlation would have a correlation coefficient of 1. In practice, most project activities have interdependencies within this range. Figure A.20 shows four scatter diagrams, illustrating correlation coefficients of 0.1, 0.3, 0.7 and 0.9.

The risk analyst should consider the common factors that affect interdependencies between project activities and select a coefficient of correlation that is appropriate, to apply either to all project activities or to specified groups of activities. (If there are a small number of groups it is usually

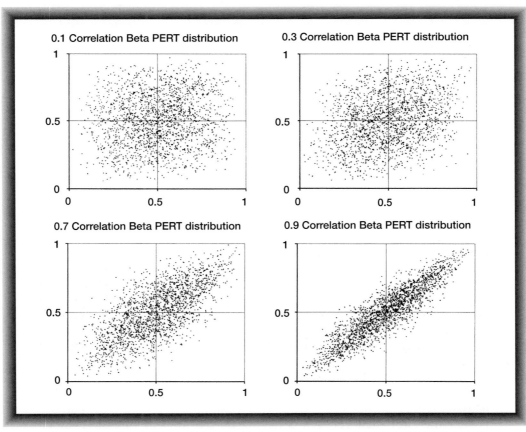

Figure A.20 *Correlation coefficients applied to a pair of symmetrical Beta PERT distributions*

reasonable to simulate the groups as being independent of one another.) The value selected for correlation coefficients should reflect the degree to which they are interrelated. Interdependencies within activity groups are likely to be stronger than interdependencies that apply to the project as a whole. Typically, experience shows that, for schedule risk analysis, correlation coefficients in the region of 0.5 are appropriate, whereas for a simple cost risk analysis, this could rise to 0.7–0.8. If the structure of the cost risk model has been designed to take into account results from the schedule analysis, then the cost model correlation coefficients should be reduced accordingly.

A3.5.3 Simulation times, numbers of iterations and Monte Carlo versus the Latin Hypercube

During a pure Monte Carlo simulation, a value for each variable is chosen at random from within the associated probability distribution. Each iteration is then truly independent of the others. One consequence is that a relatively high number of iterations have to be performed in order to avoid the possibility of results being unrealistically skewed by chance. For this reason, it is recommended that at least 2000 iterations are performed for more complex models.

Today, modern computers with suitable software can be expected to perform an analysis of 2000 iterations in an acceptably short time. However, before this was the case, practitioners sought methods to reduce the number of iterations to save time. An approach to this problem was provided by the Latin Hypercube. This method divides the probability distribution of each variable into bands and ensures that a correctly proportionate number of values are chosen from each band over the course of the number of iterations performed. The Latin Hypercube remains a legitimate short-cut to reducing the number of iterations (typically to 500), but the advent of faster computing has almost rendered it obsolete.

With modern computers, projects that have processing difficulties when running Monte Carlo models have usually made the mistake of copying their detailed plan (with thousands of activities) in order to produce their risk model. As explained earlier in this section, this is not only a fundamentally flawed approach to risk analysis, but also causes logistical difficulties in running the analysis.

A3.6 Additional techniques for presenting risk analysis results

A3.6.1 Tornado charts

Tornado charts provide a pictorial representation of a sensitivity analysis of the model. They illustrate the degree to which the uncertainty of a model's output is affected by the uncertainty of the individual variables within the model. Figure A.21 demonstrates a typical example. The longer the bar, the greater the effect that variable is having on the model's output. The bar length represents the degree of correlation between the input model variable

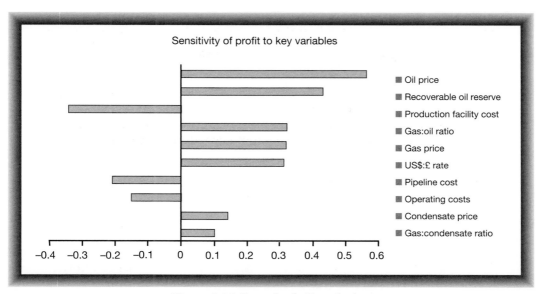

Figure A.21 *Example of a Tornado chart*

and the output. The higher the degree of correlation between the input and output variables (calculated using rank-order correlation), the more the input variable is affecting the output.

It is usual to plot the variables from the top down in decreasing size of correlation, and it is sensible to limit the number of variables that are shown on the plot. If there are positive and negative correlations, the result looks a bit like a tornado, hence the name. The Tornado chart is very useful for identifying the key uncertain variables that are driving the result of the model. If the uncertainty of these key variables can be reduced, the uncertainty of the problem will be reduced too. The Tornado chart is therefore very useful for planning any strategy for the reduction of uncertainty.

The key identified variables can often be made more certain by:

- collecting more information on the variable if the uncertainty is in the level of knowledge of the variable
- determining strategies to reduce the effect of the uncertainty of the variable. For a project schedule, this might mean altering the project plan to take the task off the critical path. For a project cost, this might mean offloading the uncertainty via a fixed-price subcontract.

A3.6.2 Spider plots

Spider plots offer another method for illustrating the effect of the individual input variables on the output's uncertainty. The variation in the input variable is shown on the x-axis against the value of the output shown on the

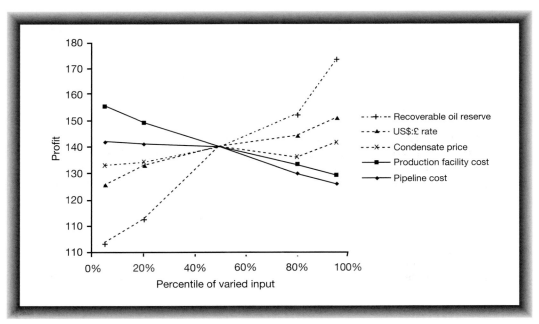

Figure A.22 *A spider plot using the same percentiles of the input variables*

y-axis. This is achieved by setting each uncertain input variable to its mean value and then changing the value of one of these inputs and noting the effect on the output. The greater the effect of the input on the output variable, the larger the vertical distance the line for that variable will cover.

The spider plot is usually shown with ± percentage changes from the mean of the input variables. Each input is set to its 50 percentile. Then, one input at a time is changed to, say, its 1, 5, 20, 80, 95 and 99 per cent values, and the resultant values of the output are noted. This second approach gives a much better quantification of the effect of the range of each input variable. Figure A.22 shows an example.

A.3.7 Decision trees

A decision tree can help when choosing the best way forward between alternative courses of action as it provides a way of formulating the problem and evaluating options. Whenever a decision must be made there are always two or more courses of action open. These can be represented as a series of 'branches' springing from a single node that represents the decision. If the value to the decision-maker of adopting each course of action can be established, then it is a simple matter to choose whichever course offers the best value. However, the identified courses of action often lead either to further decisions or uncertain outcomes. When this occurs, further branches can be drawn from the outcome of each of the original branches and the whole diagram develops a tree-like appearance – hence the title. If all the branches have potential outcomes that can be stated with a high degree of certainty then it is a straightforward matter to evaluate the overall outcome at the end of each branch, choose the most favourable one, then work backwards through the tree to establish the series of decisions that leads to the best result.

Where outcomes cannot be stated with certainty, there is a chance that whatever decision is made could turn out to be the wrong one. Decision trees can reflect this situation but, in this case, some of the branches will represent the decision options ('decision-maker's tree') and other branches will represent the outcomes determined by fate, chance or 'the state of nature' ('nature's tree'). In this situation, the rules of probability have to be applied to determine the best decision. The example below considers the problem of the project manager who has to decide whether to continue with an existing contractor who has been constantly falling behind schedule or switch to a new contractor who is promising to recover or better the schedule. Both the decision-maker's tree and nature's tree are shown in Figure A.23.

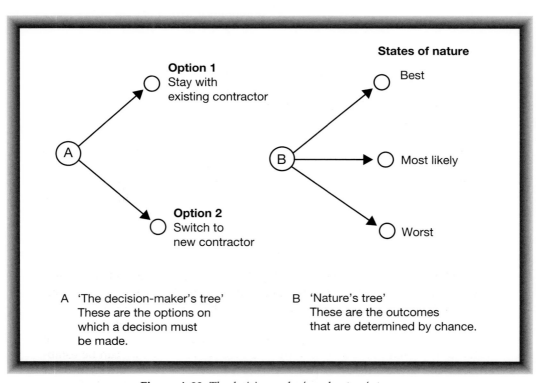

Figure A.23 *The decision-maker's and nature's trees*

Table A.4 Courses of action and possible outcomes

Courses of Action		States of Nature		
		Best (10% chance)	Most likely (70% chance)	Worst (20% chance)
Option 1 Stay with existing contractor	Outcome Cost	No slip £0	2-month slip £40K	4-month slip £80K
Option 2 Change to new contractor	Outcome Cost	1-month gain £20K	No slip £30K	1-month slip £50K

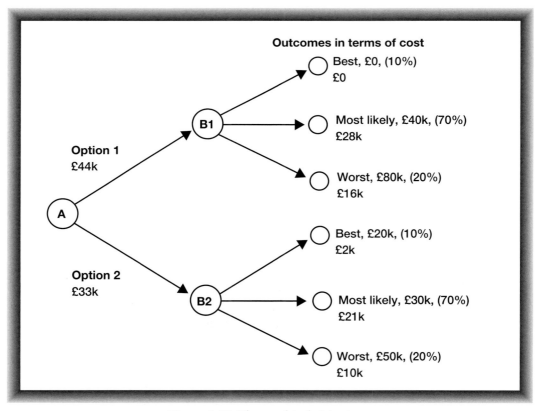

Figure A.24 *The complete decision tree*

If the likely outcomes of nature's tree and the probability of each outcome arising can be assessed, then the complete tree can be drawn and evaluated. Some data are given in Table A.4.

The decision tree resulting from the data in Table A.4, as well as the evaluation of each outcome, is shown in Figure A.24. In this figure, the decision tree has been evaluated in terms of expected costs using the rules of probability. The analysis shows that Option 2, changing to a new contractor, looks to be the better decision as it shows the lower overall expected cost (£33K as opposed to £44K for Option 1). This simple example shows the use of the decision tree for the straightforward analysis of options. However there can be situations where the decision paths, and the chance events that spring from them, can lead to increasingly divergent scenarios; in this case, finding end conditions on which to make a valid comparison of options can be difficult. Decision trees are thus best used in the simpler situations; the more complex the scenario, the less valid or less conclusive the result may be.

Glossary

This glossary defines specific terms used in the *PRAM Guide*. Risk terminology is problematic in that many practitioners and guides use similar words in a slightly different way from one another, and terms such as 'mitigation' and 'contingency' can have different meanings depending on the context and the user. This glossary confirms the definition assumed for this *Guide*.

beta distribution See *distributions*

contingency A margin of resource or specification in excess of the base estimate (for example, of money available for the conduct of the project, of float within the initial project plan, of overspecification of product characteristics) to enable the achievement of project objectives in the face of the impact of specific risk events. See also *provisions*.

contingency planning business case A justification for the allocation of project resource to a particular *risk response*. In general, the cost of the response (in time and/or money) will be justified on the basis of a reduction or elimination of a threat, or realisation of an opportunity, bearing in mind both the probability and impact of the threat or opportunity. The business case may not be based entirely on money or time, as unquantifiable impacts, such as health and safety or corporate reputation, may be an important part of the impact assessment.

contractual strategies *Risk responses* that limit and/or manage the allocation of risk across commercial boundaries by defining responsibilities and consequences between the parties to the contract. The scope for managing risk in this way is limited severely once the contract is agreed and signed.

distributions A characteristic statistical pattern of occurrences of values for a particular outcome when repeated many times. In statistical modelling, values are generated within a defined range according to particular distribution, thought to be representative of the value being modelled. Normal, uniform, beta and negative exponential are examples of distributions. Each of these distributions have characteristic shapes when values are plotted against frequency of occurrence. For example, a normal distribution has a bell shape, exponential curves from horizontal to vertical and uniform has a straight horizontal line.

fallback plan See *reactive risk response*.

force majeure risks Low-probability risks with a high impact on the project, usually arising from causes outside the project's sphere of influence – for example, catastrophic environmental conditions, disturbance of normal working conditions or prevention or suspension of operations. Force majeure risks are difficult to manage within a project and are often escalated to a higher level.

impact The effect on the project objectives if the risk event should occur.

mitigation The term 'mitigation' is often used to refer to all responses to threats but some practitioners use the term to refer specifically to proactive risk responses and others specifically to reactive risk responses.

Monte Carlo sampling method A method of simulation modelling using a large number of random samples across the range of the distribution. Latin Hypercube is an alternative sampling method using stratified sampling. Latin Hypercube tends to result in convergence of the model using fewer samples.

opportunity An upside, beneficial source of risk.

PERT A representation of a set of activities showing task, duration and dependency information, usually depicted as a network diagram. PERT (Programme Evaluation and Review Technique) was developed in the 1950s to address the problems of complex project scheduling.

probabilistic models Mathematical models combining several uncertain values and uncertain events to derive a range of possible outcomes. Probabilistic models generally use *Monte Carlo sampling methods*.

probability-impact matrices A representation of a portfolio of risks plotted in two dimensions – probability and impact. Probability-impact matrices can be used to prioritise risk management activities and monitor the success (or otherwise) of risk management activities.

phases The phases and sub-phases of the risk management process are as follows.
1 *Initiate*, in which the scope, objectives and context for the process is defined. The Initiate phase comprises two sub-phases, *Define Project* and *Focus Risk Management Process*.
   - *Define Project* consolidates information about the project in a form suitable for risk management and fills any gaps in that information.
   - *Focus Risk Management Process* defines the aims of the risk management process for this project (or stage) and plans how those aims will be achieved and the resources, tools and practices required.
2 *Identify*, in which the risk events relevant to the project are identified as comprehensively as possible. Several tools and techniques are available to facilitate risk identification
3 *Assess* in which further information is gathered about each identified risk and the level of overall project risk. Assessment will include estimating the *probability* and *impact* of specific risks, the *risk impact window* and the combined effect of risks. Assessment may use both *quantitative assessment* and *qualitative assessment*.

The Assess phase has four sub-phases, Structure, Ownership, Estimate and Evaluate.

- *Structure* defines the relationship between risk events and between events and responses, to enable more effective responses to be made.
- *Ownership* defines responsibility for managing the risk and each of the responses, both within the project and across contractual boundaries.
- *Estimate* deals with techniques for the quantification of the risk impacts and probabilities, bearing in mind the quality and reliability of the source data.
- *Evaluate* examines the combined effect of the uncertainty from individual risks, applying appropriate techniques to identify risk-efficient responses.

4 *Plan Responses*, in which responses to individual risk events, and to the overall project risk, are determined. These aims may be addressed together in the Plan Responses phase, or as two sub-phases, *Plan Risk Event Responses* and *Plan Project Risk Responses*.

- *Plan Risk Event Responses* ensures that all risk responses are cost-effective and practical and that triggers are defined, approved and agreed with the owners.
- *Plan Project Risk Responses* considers the combined effect of specific responses, and the identification of general responses associated with the collective management of overall risk.

5 *Implement Responses*, in which actions identified during the Plan Responses phase are carried out.

6 *Manage Process*, which is concerned with monitoring effectiveness and controlling progress of the risk process itself, and ensuring that the requirements and deliverables of the risk management plan are met.

These phases are explained in more detail in Chapter 4.

PRAM Project Risk Analysis and Management.

proactive risk response An action or set of actions to reduce the probability or impact of a *threat* (or delay its occurrence), or increase the probability or impact of an *opportunity* (or bring forward its occurrence). Proactive risk responses, if approved, are carried out in advance of the occurrence of the risk. They are funded from the project budget.

probability An estimate of the likelihood that a particular risk event will occur, usually expressed on a scale of 0 to 1 or 0 to 100 per cent. In a project context, estimates of probability are often subjective, as the combination of tasks, people and other circumstances is usually unique. In a controlled, repeatable environment, such as a factory or laboratory, it may be possible to derive objective probabilities such as fault rates.

probability distribution See *distributions*.

probability distribution shapes See *distributions*.

project life cycle The phases through which most projects pass from initial idea to closure. These phases may be summarised as conception, feasibility, implementation, operation and termination. The extent, nature and potential treatment of risk at each of these phases may be different.

project objectives A statement of specific and measurable aims by which the degree of success of the project will be assessed.

project risk The exposure of stakeholders to the consequences of variations in outcome. The overall risk affecting the whole project, defined by components associated with risk events, other sources of uncertainty and associated dependencies, to be managed at a strategic level.

provisions Time, money or other resources that are made available to cover variation from target value or estimate, not arising from a specific risk event. Provisions will be used on average, whilst contingencies will be used in exceptional cases – when a risk event occurs. See also *contingency*.

qualitative assessment An assessment of risk relating to the qualities and subjective elements of the risk – those that cannot be quantified accurately. Qualitative techniques include the definition of risk, the recording of risk details and relationships, and the categorisation and prioritisation of risks relative to each other.

quantitative analysis Modelling of numerical outcomes by combining actual or estimated values with an assumed or known relationship between values, using arithmetic or statistical techniques, to determine a range of likely outcomes of a variable or to understand how variance in one or more values is likely to affect others.

reactive risk response An action or set of actions to be taken after a risk event has occurred (as defined by the *trigger condition*) in order to reduce or address the effect of the threat, or maximise the effect of the opportunity. The cost of reactive risk responses is met from *contingency*.

risk efficiency The minimum level of project risk for a given level of expected performance.

risk event An uncertain event or set of circumstances that, should it or they occur, would have an effect on the achievement of one or more of the project's objectives.

risk analysis Assessment and synthesis of the risks affecting a project to gain an understanding of their individual significance and their combined *impact* on the project's objectives, as a basis for determining priorities for the application of *risk responses*.

risk impact window The time during which the risk *impact* may occur. This is of use in prioritising the *risk response* and phasing *contingency* over the timescale of the project.

risk management The process whereby *project risk* is understood and responses to the *risk events* are formulated, justified, planned, initiated, progressed, monitored, measured for success, reviewed, adjusted and closed.

risk management maturity A measure of the extent to which a project or organisation formally applies effective and efficient risk management to support decision-making and the treatment of risk.

risk management plan A document defining how *risk management* is to be implemented in the context of the particular project concerned.

risk register A body of information containing all the risks identified for the project; also explaining the nature of each risk and recording information relevant to its assessment and management.

risk response Action to reduce the exposure to risk. For a *threat*, the response aims to reduce the probability of the threat arising or to reduce the significance of its detrimental impact if it were to arise. For an *opportunity*, the response aims to increase the probability of an opportunity arising and to increase the significance of its beneficial impact.

   Risk responses can be *proactive* or *reactive*.

risk response window The time during which the *risk response* will be effective. This is of use in planning and prioritising the risk response and phasing *contingency* over the timescale of the project.

secondary risk event A *risk event* that may occur as a result of invoking a *risk response* or *fallback plan*.

sensitivity analysis A technique that seeks to examine the sensitivity of model results to parameter estimates. Simple forms include varying parameters one at a time and observing the effect in order to inform decisions. A useful form for *risk management* involves the use of diagrams such as Figure 4.3 (p. 37) to portray the *impact* of all parameters defining a set of related probability *distributions* in a direct manner.

stakeholder An individual or organisation that has an effect on, or could be affected by, the outcome of the project.

statistical dependence An observed correlation between one value and another in a probabilistic model indicating a possible causal link between the two values represented.

sub-phase See *phases*.

threat A source of downside, adverse risk.

trigger condition A definition of the circumstances in which a risk is deemed to have occurred, or upon which a fallback action will be initiated.

Further Reading

BOOKS

Bartlett, J., 2002. *Managing Risk for Projects and Programmes: A Risk Handbook.* Published by Project Manager Today Publications, Hook, Hampshire, UK. ISBN 1900391104.

Bernstein, P.L., 1996. *Against the Gods – The Remarkable Story of Risk.* Published by J. Wiley, Chichester, UK. ISBN 0471121045.

Boehm, B.W., 1989. *Software Risk Management.* Published by IEEE Computer Society Press, Piscataway, New Jersey, USA. ISBN 0818689064.

Chapman, C.B. and Ward, S.C., 2003. *Project Risk Management: Processes, Techniques and Insights.* Published by J. Wiley, Chichester, UK. ISBN 0470853557.

Chapman, C.B. and Ward, S.C., 2002. *Managing Project Risk and Uncertainty: A Constructively Simple Approach to Decision Making.* Published by J. Wiley, Chichester, UK. ISBN 0470847905.

Charette, R.N., 1989. *Software Engineering Risk Analysis and Management.* Published by McGraw-Hill, New York, USA. ISBN 007010719X.

Dorofee, A.J. *et al.*, 1996. *Continuous Risk Management Guidebook.* Published by SEI Carnegie Mellon University, USA.

Edwards, L., 1995. *Practical Risk Management in the Construction Industry.* Published by Thomas Telford. ISBN 0727720643.

Flyvbjerg, B., Bruzelius, N. and Rothengatter, W., 2003. *Megaprojects and Risk: An Anatomy of Ambition.* Published by Cambridge University Press, Cambridge, UK. ISBN 0521804205.

Godfrey, P.S., 1995. *Control of Risk: A Guide to the Systematic Management of Risk from Construction.* Published by CIRIA under reference FR/CP/32.

Grey, S., 1995. *Practical Risk Assessment for Project Management.* Published by J. Wiley, Chichester, UK. ISBN 047193978X.

Hall, E.M., 1998. *Managing Risk – Methods for Software Systems Development.* Published by Addison Wesley Longman, Reading, MA, USA. ISBN 0201255928.

Hillson, D.A., 2003. *Effective Opportunity Management for Projects: Exploiting Positive Risk.* Published by Marcel Dekker, New York, USA.

HM Government Cabinet Office Strategy Unit, 2002. 'Risk: Improving Government's Capability to Handle Risk and Uncertainty. Report ref. 254205/1102/D16, Crown copyright 2002.

Kähkönen, K. and Artto, K.A. (eds), 1997. 'Managing Risks in Projects'. Published by E & FN Spon. ISBN 0419229906.

Kahneman, D., Slovic, P. and Tversky, A. (eds) 1986. *Judgement under Uncertainty: Heuristics and Biases*. Published by Cambridge University Press, Cambridge, UK.

Kliem, R.L. and Ludin, I.S., 1997. *Reducing Project Risk*. Published by Gower, Aldershot, UK. ISBN 056607799X.

Pritchard, C., 2001. *Risk Management: Concepts and Guidance*. Published by ESI International. ISBN 189036701X.

Vose, D., 2000. *Risk Analysis – A Quantitative Guide* (second edition). Published by J. Wiley, Chichester, UK. ISBN 047199765X.

Williams, T.M., 2002. *Modelling Complex Projects*. Published by J. Wiley, Chichester, UK. ISBN 0471899453.

Yates, J.F. (ed.), 1992. *Risk-taking Behaviour*. Published by J. Wiley, Chichester, UK. ISBN 0471922501.

ARTICLES

Chapman, C.B. and Ward, S.C., 2000. 'Estimation and evaluation of uncertainty – a minimalist first-pass approach'. *International Journal of Project Management*, Volume 18, Number 6, pp. 369–383.

Cooke-Davies, T., 1998. 'Can we afford to skimp on risk management?' *Project Manager Today*, Volume 10, Issue 9, pp. 12–15.

de Cano, A. and de la Cruz, M.P., 1998. 'The past, present and future of project risk management'. *International Journal of Project and Business Risk Management*, Volume 2, Issue 4, pp. 361–387.

Hillson, D.A., 1997. 'Towards a risk maturity model'. *International Journal of Project and Business Risk Management*, Volume 1, Issue 1, pp. 35–45.

Hillson, D.A., 2002. 'Extending the risk process to manage opportunities'. *International Journal of Project Management*, Volume 20, Number 3, pp. 235–240.

Hillson, D.A., 2002. 'Using the risk breakdown structure (RBS) to understand risks'. *Proceedings of the 33rd Annual Project Management Institute Seminars and Symposium* (PMI 2002), presented in San Antonio, USA, 7–8 October 2002.

Hillson, D.A., 2000. 'Project risks – identifying causes, risks and effects'. *PM Network*, Volume 14, Number 9, pp. 48–51.

Hopkinson, M., 2000. 'The risk maturity model'. *Risk Management Bulletin*, Volume 5, Issue 4, pp. 25–29.

McCray, G.E., Purvis, R.L. and McCray, C.G., 2002. 'Project management under uncertainty: the impact of heuristics and biases'. *Project Management Journal*, Volume 33, Number 1, pp. 49–57.

Raz, T. and Michael, E., 2001. 'Use and benefits of tools for project risk management'. *International Journal of Project Management*, Volume 19, Number 1, pp. 9–17.

Tversky, A. and Kahneman, D., 1974. 'Judgement under uncertainty: heuristics and biases'. *Science*, Volume 185, pp. 1124–1131.

Ward, S.C. and Chapman, C.B., 1991. 'Extending the use of risk analysis in project management'. *International Journal of Project Management*, Volume 9, Number 2, pp. 117–123.

Ward, S.C. and Chapman, C.B., 2003. 'Transforming project risk management into project uncertainty management'. *International Journal of Project Management*, Volume 21, Number 2, pp. 97–105.

Williams, T.M., 1994. 'Using the risk register to integrate risk management in project definition'. *International Journal of Project Management*, Volume 12, pp. 17–22.

Williams, T.M., 1996. 'The two-dimensionality of project risk'. *International Journal of Project Management*, Volume 14, pp. 185–186.

STANDARDS

Australian/New Zealand Standard AS/NZS 4360:1999. *Risk management.* Published jointly by Standards Australia, Homebush NSW 2140, Australia, and Standards New Zealand, Wellington 6001, New Zealand. ISBN 073372647X.

British Standard BS6079-1:2002. *Project Management – Part 1: Guide to Project Management.* Published by British Standards Institute, London, UK. ISBN 0580397165.

British Standard BS6079-2:2000. *Project Management – Part 2: Vocabulary.* Published by British Standards Institute, London, UK. ISBN 0580331482.

British Standard BS6079-3:2000. *Project Management – Part 3: Guide to the Management of Business-related Project Risk.* Published by British Standards Institute, London, UK. ISBN 0580331229.

British Standard BS8444-3:1996 (IEC 300-3-9: 1995). *Risk Management: Part 3 – Guide to Risk Analysis of Technological Systems.* Published by British Standards Institute, London, UK. ISBN 0580261107.

BS IEC 62198:2001. *Project Risk Management – Application Guidelines.* Published by British Standards Institute, London, UK. ISBN 0580390195.

BSI PD 6668:2000. *Managing Risk for Corporate Governance.* Published by British Standards Institute, London, UK. ISBN 0580332462.

BSI PD ISO/IEC Guide 73:2002. *Risk Management – Vocabulary – Guidelines for Use in Standards.* Published by British Standards Institute, London, UK. ISBN 0580401782.

Institute of Chartered Accountants in England and Wales (ICAEW) 1999. *Internal Control: Guidance for Directors on the Combined Code.* Published by ICAEW, London UK. ISBN 1841520101.

Institution of Civil Engineers (ICE) and Faculty & Institute of Actuaries 1997. *Risk Analysis and Management for Projects (RAMP).* Published by Thomas Telford. ISBN 0727726978.

National Standard of Canada CAN/CSA-Q850-97. *Risk Management: Guideline for Decision-makers.* Published by Canadian Standards Association, Ontario, Canada. ISSN 0317-5669.

Norges Standardiseringsforbund (NSF) 1991. Norsk Standard NS5814:1991. *Krav til risikoanalyser.*

Project Management Institute 2000. *A Guide to the Project Management Body of Knowledge* (*PMBoK®*) (2000 edition). Project Management Institute, Philadelphia, USA. ISBN 1880410257 (CD-ROM).

UK Office of Government Commerce (OGC) 2002. *Management of Risk – Guidance for Practitioners*. Published by The Stationery Office, London, UK. ISBN 0113309090.

Index

Index

Index